BALANCING THE SCALES OF OPPORTUNITY

Ensuring Racial and Ethnic Diversity in the Health Professions

Committee on Increasing Minority Participation
in the Health Professions

Marion Ein Lewin and Barbara Rice, Editors

Office of Health Policy Programs and Fellowships

INSTITUTE OF MEDICINE

NATIONAL ACADEMY PRESS
Washington, D.C. 1994

NATIONAL ACADEMY PRESS • 2101 Constitution Avenue, N.W. • Washington, D.C. 20418

NOTICE: The project that is the subject of this report was approved by the Governing Board of the National Research Council, whose members are drawn from the councils of the National Academy of Sciences, the National Academy of Engineering, and the Institute of Medicine. The members of the committee responsible for the report were chosen for their special competences and with regard for appropriate balance.

This report has been reviewed by a group other than the authors according to procedures approved by a Report Review Committee consisting of members of the National Academy of Sciences, the National Academy of Engineering, and the Institute of Medicine.

The Institute of Medicine was chartered in 1970 by the National Academy of Sciences to enlist distinguished members of the appropriate professions in the examination of policy matters pertaining to the health of the public. In this, the Institute acts under both the Academy's 1863 congressional charter responsibility to be an adviser to the federal government and its own initiative in identifying issues of medical care, research, and education. Dr. Kenneth I. Shine is president of the Institute of Medicine.

Support for this project was provided by The Josiah Macy, Jr., Foundation (Grant No. S91711), The Robert Wood Johnson Foundation (Grant No. 18530), The Pew Charitable Trusts (Grant No. 91-01994-000), and the Office of Special Populations, National Institute of Mental Health, U.S. Department of Health and Human Services (Grant No. 92MF34075601D).

Library of Congress Catalog Card No. 94-66070
International Standard Book No. 0-309-05078-2

Additional copies of this book are available from the National Academy Press, 2101 Constitution Avenue, N.W., Box 285, Washington, D.C. 20055. Call 800-624-6242 or 202-334-3313 (in the Washington Metropolitan Area).

B333

Copyright 1994 by the National Academy of Sciences. All rights reserved.

Printed in the United States of America

The serpent has been a symbol of long life, healing, and knowledge among almost all cultures and religions since the beginning of recorded history. The image adopted as a logotype by the Institute of Medicine is based on a relief carving from ancient Greece, now held by the Staatlichemuseen in Berlin.

COMMITTEE TO INCREASE MINORITY PARTICIPATION IN THE HEALTH PROFESSIONS

M. ALFRED HAYNES,[*] *Chair*, Formerly of Drew University of Medicine and Science, Los Angeles, California
JOAN BARATZ-SNOWDEN, National Board for Professional Teaching Standards, Washington, D.C.
THOMAS L. DELBANCO, Harvard Medical School and Beth Israel Hospital, Boston, Massachusetts
JUANITA W. FLEMING,[*] Academic Affairs, University of Kentucky, Lexington, Kentucky
JAMES R. GAVIN III, Howard Hughes Medical Institute, Bethesda, Maryland
GERALD HILL, Center of American Indian and Minority Health, University of Minnesota School of Medicine, Duluth, Minnesota
JAMES JENNINGS, William Monroe Trotter Institute, University of Massachusetts, Boston, Massachusetts
LEON JOHNSON, JR., National Medical Fellowships, Inc., New York, New York
DEIDRE DUMAS LABAT, College of Arts and Sciences, Xavier University, New Orleans, Louisiana
TANYA PAGAN RAGGIO, Healthy Start, Inc., Pittsburgh, Pennsylvania
DAVID J. SANCHEZ, JR., Academic Affairs/Academic Programs, University of California at San Francisco, San Francisco, California
EDWARD J. STEMMLER,[*] Association of American Medical Colleges, Washington, D.C.

STUDY STAFF

Office of Health Policy Programs and Fellowships

MARION EIN LEWIN, *Study Director*
JO HARRIS-WEHLING, *Program Officer*
VALERIE TATE, *Program Assistant*
COIMBRA SIRICA, *Writer*
BARBARA RICE, *Editor*

---

[*] Institute of Medicine Member

Preface

The report *Balancing the Scales of Opportunity: Ensuring Racial and Ethnic Diversity in the Health Professions*, was initiated in response to numerous requests from the membership of the Institute of Medicine (IOM), including several members serving on the Institute's Council and Program Committee, to reassess underrepresentation of minorities in the health professions in light of impending health care reform and its implications for the nation's future workforce. The leadership of the Association of Academic Minority Physicians and the National Cancer Institute of the National Institutes of Health also encouraged the Institute to undertake this kind of effort.

While recently published data indicate a significant upturn in the number of minorities entering medical school, an enrollment goal of 12 percent set by the Association of American Medical Colleges in the mid-1970s still remains elusive. Minorities enrolled in medical schools reached only 10.3 percent in 1992, although these groups represent 22.1 percent of the U.S. population. Underrepresentation in the health professions is even more disturbing when one looks at the paltry number of minority faculty. In 1992, they made up only 3.5 percent of faculty members in medical schools.

Interest in the study came amidst an increasing sense of crisis about the U.S. health care system, particularly the widening gap in health status between majority and minority populations. These pressing concerns were being viewed within the broader context of a changing demographic landscape and the importance of giving greater attention to the health and social needs of America's fastest growing population groups: African Americans, Hispanics, and Native Americans. Underlying these trends was the growing realization that our nation would not be able to thrive in the twenty-first century without a willingness to recognize, stimulate, and develop the capacities of all segments of society and to acknowledge the needs of those groups currently underrepresented in health careers.

These new and powerful dynamics stimulated the IOM, with its long interest and commitment to improving the quality and context of our health care system, to appoint a committee that would help to develop a future-oriented action and research agenda for enhancing minority participation in the health professions. The 12 members chosen for the committee represented a range of views on medical and science education, health professions training, minority recruitment, retention, outreach programs, and medical education financing. Funding for the study came from three foundations and one government organization well-recognized for their interest and commitment to this issue: The Macy Foundation; The Robert Wood Johnson Foundation; The Pew Charitable Trusts; and the Office of Special Populations, the National Institute of Mental Health.

The committee was charged with three tasks:

1. to develop a future-oriented research and strategic action agenda, responsive to the realities of the 1990s;
2. to focus on multiple aspects of professional development that affect participation of underrepresented minorities in the health professions, such as education, academic achievement, opportunity, and mentoring; and
3. to address the "health professions" (in as much as resources allow) from a global, broadly defined perspective, with a more targeted focus on minority participation in clinical practice and academic medicine.

The undertaking of original data analysis was beyond the scope of the committee. However, an extensive literature search of data findings, past activities, evaluations, and related information was conducted.

As the centerpiece of its study effort, the committee convened an invitational workshop to discuss ways in which the country can enhance the presence of minority participation in the health professions. Twenty-four participants from across the nation were invited, representing a wide range of backgrounds and experiences in this arena. Participants were invited on the basis of their noted contributions to the field of minority education and advancement, as health professionals, educators, community leaders, and researchers. The group was challenged to think broadly and creatively about developing strategic future directions for helping more minority Americans realize their capacities in professional health careers.

During a day and a half of interactive dialogue and small group discussion, workshop participants identified obstacles and the promising strategies and approaches for ensuring the greater participation of minorities in the health professions. The workshop discussions were informed and guided in part by several formal papers commissioned by the committee. These papers included the following:

- "Inventory and Analysis of the Effectiveness of Strategies and Programs for Increasing Minority Participation in Medicine" by Timothy Ready and Herbert Nickens.
- "Educational and Career Obstacles and Opportunities in Academic Medicine and Clinical Practice for Priorities: Is Progress Occurring?" by Louis Cregler, Luther Clark, and Edgar Jackson.
- "Increasing Minority Participation in the Health Professions—The Problem of Underrepresentation and an Inventory and Analysis of Effective Strategies and Programs" by A. Cherrie Epps, Mary Cureton-Russell, and Helen Kitzman.

During the workshop deliberations the committee used several terms requiring definition: African American, participation, minority, and health professions. Although the term "African American" can be used to refer to only one sector in the broader black community, the committee made a deliberate decision to include all groups of African descent; thus, the term is meant to include West Indians and Africans, as well as those black groups who have lived in the United States since its founding. While there are recognized differences among subgroups of all the ethnic minorities discussed in this report, the committee preferred not to subdivide the groups, and especially not to make a distinction on the basis of country of origin.

By "participation" the committee covered all areas of the health professions: clinical service, teaching, or research within any health profession. Furthermore, full participation means that minorities will have equal opportunities to fulfill their potential without barriers based on race or ethnicity.

The committee was aware of different ways of defining "minorities" and of increasing pressure from racial and ethnic groups not presently included as "underrepresented minorities." For this reason the committee chose definitions specifically for the purposes of this study. By "minorities" the committee means African Americans, Hispanics, and Native Americans. These groups are the focus of this study not only because they are markedly underrepresented in the health professions, but also because they are a statistical minority that has a documented group history of deprivation in U.S. society. Large numbers of these groups have historically and systematically been excluded from admission to educational institutions or from professional employment opportunities because of their "racial" identity or because they were ill prepared, when the lack of preparation was in large measure due to being a member of a minority group. The committee explored the reasons for the underrepresentation and considered strategies that have made or could make a real difference in outcomes.

By "health professions" the committee intended to include the major healing professions such as medicine, dentistry, and nursing. However, more data are available on medicine than on the other professions. To the extent problems are similar, it is possible to draw broader conclusions based on the more adequate data on physicians.

Although all three ethnic groups are the focus of attention, the report provides more data on African Americans simply because more data are available on this group. Data routinely collected by the Association of American Medical Colleges (AAMC) include information about African Americans, Native Americans, Mexican Americans, and mainland Puerto Ricans. Other health professions do not have a similar database, although Hispanic and Native American scholars could assist in developing a more useful database if resources were available. Data on Hispanics represent a special challenge due to differences in definitions that make it impossible to reconcile data from different sources (IOM, 1993). For the purpose of this study, the AAMC's categorization is used.

The committee's report contains an Executive Summary, with key observations and recommendations; four chapters; and two appendixes. Chapter 1 describes the rationale for the study and the significance of the problem. Chapter 2 presents data that help to define the problem of underrepresentation and identifies underlying factors that contribute to the failure to achieve desired societal goals. Chapter 3 provides information on programs that illustrate various attempts to solve the problems identified in Chapter 2. In Chapter 4, the committee proposes a number of strategies developed at the workshop. These strategies are intended to grasp the opportunities inherent in the current climate of change and to ensure a greatly increased and continuous flow of qualified minority health professionals prepared to meet the challenges of the future. Finally, Appendix A contains the lists of participants and commissioned papers for the workshop, and Appendix B provides the names of additional organizations and publications that focus on the committee's concerns.

M. Alfred Haynes, M.D.
Chair

Acknowledgments

I want to take this opportunity to thank my colleagues on the committee for their dedication and extremely hard work. As a committee we wish to acknowledge the individuals who led and participated in the workshop and who gave so generously of their time to help enrich our study (see Appendix A). In addition, the committee wants to express special appreciation to the primary authors of the commissioned papers: Louis Cregler, A. Cherrie Epps, Herbert Nickens, and Timothy Ready. The thoughtful and informative background papers enhanced our understanding of the many dimensions of this complex issue.

The committee wishes to recognize the substantial help that it received from various individuals at the American Association for the Advancement of Science, the National Science Foundation, the Association of American Medical Colleges, Education West, and the Health Careers Opportunity Program of the Department of Health and Human Services. We owe a debt of gratitude to National Medical Fellowships, Inc. for its inspiration for the report's title.

The committee wants to give special thanks to the dedicated and hard-working professional staff at the Institute of Medicine: study director Marion Ein Lewin; program officer Jo Harris-Wehling; program assistant Valerie Tate; and program associate Karen Orlando. Coimbra Sirica had the difficult task of assuming some major writing responsibilities midstream. Barbara Rice deserves many thanks for her excellent editing, managing to integrate a variety of ideas and writing styles. We are especially grateful to them.

Contents

EXECUTIVE SUMMARY		1
1	**INTRODUCTION**	11
	Background, 11	
	Significance of the Problem, 14	
2	**FACTORS THAT DEFINE THE PIPELINE**	21
	Where the Leak Begins, 26	
	Factors Associated with Minority Underrepresentation, 38	
	Conclusion, 45	
3	**LESSONS FROM SUCCESSFUL PROGRAMS**	46
	Medical School Level, 46	
	Postbaccalaureate Programs, 48	
	College Programs, 49	
	University Outreach, 52	
	High School Program, 54	
	Comprehensive Programs, 54	
	Summary, 56	
4	**SHARING VISIONS AND WORKING TOWARD THE FUTURE**	58
	Building the Vision, 61	
	Moving the Vision Forward, 71	
	Summary, 74	
REFERENCES		76
APPENDIX A: LISTING OF WORKSHOP PARTICIPANTS AND COMMISSIONED PAPERS		82
APPENDIX B: FURTHER SOURCES OF INFORMATION		85

Executive Summary

BACKGROUND

The underrepresentation of minorities in the health and other professions has long cast a shadow over our nation's efforts to develop a more representative and productive society. Many laudable and durable programs have been developed over the past 20 years to enlarge the presence of minorities in health careers, but these efforts have been unable to develop the infrastructure and momentum to produce and sustain an adequate number of minority professionals among the ranks of America's clinicians, researchers, and teachers. While there has been an increase in the numbers of African Americans, Hispanics, and Native Americans enrolled in professional schools during the past decade, this increase remains well below their representation in the population. Minorities in the health professions are more underrepresented today than 15 years ago.

In 1992, underrepresented minorities in medical schools reached 10.3 percent of total enrollment, reflecting a hopeful upward trend after many years of thwarted progress. Nevertheless, these groups, represent over 22 percent of the U.S. population, a percentage that is expected to grow to 25 percent by the year 2000. Underrepresentation is even more disturbing when one looks at the small number of minorities among the nation's health professions faculty and researchers. The percentage of underrepresented medical school minority faculty in 1992 was 3.5 percent; only one-third of U.S. medical schools have 4 percent or more of their faculty who are underrepresented minorities.

These concerns are not new. For more than 25 years, many individuals and institutions have shared a common vision for enhancing the participation of minorities in all aspects of health care, and many resources have been directed toward achieving this goal. Major social forces and strong political leadership helped to bring about the increases in minority enrollment in the health professions that began in 1968. At that time, the climate of the Civil Rights era and economic prosperity in the United States converged, and the nation seemed poised to commit itself to overcoming the barriers to full participation by minorities in the health professions.

The promise, however, was not fulfilled. Progress in matriculating minorities came to a virtual halt in the mid-1970s, particularly in medicine, which had been at the forefront of earlier efforts to educate minority students.

No one can point to the sole reason for the persistent underrepresentation and stalled progress that began in the late 1970s. Some of the loss of momentum has been attributed to a slower economy, rising deficits, a diminished domestic agenda, and declining interest in providing educational support in the form of scholarships to minority students—in part a response to a broadly publicized study produced in the 1980s, which predicted an oversupply of health care professionals by the year 2000.

Minority students also report an insidious set of less tangible barriers—both academic and social—that stood in the way of educational advancement and the pursuit of a health professions career: denial of access to quality education; teachers who expect too little of students; anti-intellectual peer pressure; and a cultural gap between the world of study and that of their families and neighborhoods. Even significant efforts by government agencies, leading foundations, and a number of committed institutions were not successful in building the institutional and academic infrastructure necessary to eliminate the gap between vision and reality. Past efforts have yielded only marginal gains, occasional snapshots of steps forward that have not developed into a lasting picture of significant and sustained progress.

Today the issue of revitalizing the agenda for broadening the landscape of minority participation in health careers has a new urgency and relevance that go beyond past calls for social equality and justice. Compelling demographic trends alone speak to the value and wisdom of broadening educational opportunities for minorities to pursue careers in medicine as well as other professional callings that contribute so much to a nation's strength and productivity. Minorities are increasing faster than the rest of the population. By the year 2020, 40 percent of America's youth will be members of minority groups. Policymakers have expressed concern about future productivity across most U.S. industries, including health, unless we can adopt policies that support the development of human resources within our increasingly diverse ethnic populations.

Mounting social and political pressures in support of major reform of the nation's health care system add yet another dimension of timeliness and urgency to the issue of enhanced minority representation in clinical practice and teaching. Some of the most serious deficiencies in our current health care enterprise are reflected in the growing disparity in health status between minority and majority populations. While a host of factors—socioeconomic, genetic, cultural, and institutional—determine an individual's health status and use of health care services, a starting point to improving minority access may be to increase the

EXECUTIVE SUMMARY

supply of minority physicians. Data and information do illustrate that minority physicians show a greater tendency to practice in their communities or other underserved areas. Further, minorities practicing medicine, teaching classes, and conducting research with other health professionals can lead to more empathetic communication and health care for minority patients and patients in general. Indeed, the Clinton administration's plan for health care reform calls for the "creation of a new health workforce" and enhanced investment in "recruiting and supporting the education of health professionals from population groups underrepresented in the field." There is every indication that any reform strategy will provide incentives for enlarging the ranks of primary caregivers, nurses, and allied health professionals who enter community practice, a focus that represents promising career opportunities for minorities.

Within this context of dynamic and exciting change, the committee saw a bright opportunity to assess past programs and policies in order to identify those strategies that can help lead to a more effective and sustained agenda for enhancing the participation of minorities in the health professions. To meet the needs for health care, education, and research in an increasingly diverse society, the committee tried to formulate a strategy that would ensure significant growth and a continuous supply of minority health professionals. The committee discussed a future health professions workforce that looks more like America, where clinicians, researchers, and teachers increasingly reflect the cultural and ethnic diversity that has contributed so much to our nation and holds the key to its future. The committee approached the study from the perspective of enriching the current and future ethnic mix of health professionals rather than adding to the overall numbers.

MAJOR FINDINGS AND RECOMMENDATIONS

The committee's major findings and recommendations focus on the need for a more systematic, strategic, and sustained approach to ensure the continuous flow of minority students qualified to choose careers in the health professions. Any substantial improvement in minority health professions school enrollment can occur only if the pipeline is broadened and more minority students are given the opportunity for solid academic preparation in a supportive environment, beginning even before high school.

Findings

- *A critical aspect of the committee's findings points to the need to place greater emphasis on the "throughput" of the educational process and on programs that will significantly increase the number of minorities prepared academically to pursue careers in medicine and science.*

The goal must be to recruit minority students to science early and to maintain and support them as they pass through the pipeline so that they are better prepared for admission to professional training, thus ensuring that they will graduate and be well established toward a professional career.

A fundamental cause of the underrepresentation of minorities in the health professions is an inadequate number of academically qualified and nearly qualified students interested in health careers. Many past programs and strategies have relied too heavily on supplementary enrichment and recruiting programs for advanced premedical and postgraduate students. They have failed to address the root cause—the need to develop the applicant pool at earlier stages of the educational process. Further, a greater presence of minorities in clinical practice and research will not be achieved by looking at the field of medicine alone. Sustained and concerted strategies to enlarge the pool must include the other health professions as well, including dentistry, optometry, pharmacy, podiatric medicine, veterinary medicine, nursing, and the growing field of allied health.

- *The committee calls for the development of intervention programs that emphasize more systematic, integrated strategies to ensure a continuous flow of minority students qualified to choose careers in the health professions.*

Only by moving away from ancillary activities aimed at helping students survive the current educational climate to changing the climate in which students are educated, can we significantly affect the participation of minorities in health science careers. Collaboration and linkages among all levels of the institutions and organizations related to the educational process must characterize future efforts to increase minority participation in the health professions. Improvements at each point affect all other points. The weak links among elementary school, high school, college, and graduate school place our students at greatest risk.

- *The committee encourages education reform that stresses a strong science and math foundation.*

In recent years it has become clear that the quality and quantity of mathematical and science instruction given to students throughout their academic lives determine how prepared they will be for science-based careers. Data show, however, that students of all races filter out of science and math, so that only a fraction of interested high school students go on to earn advanced degrees in these disciplines. The minority pipeline, smaller to begin with, narrows even more sharply than that of the total population. To reverse this trend, effective strategies must focus on making science and mathematics more accessible to all students, especially to minorities and women. Establishing these competencies early in the educational process will help develop a cadre of minorities qualified to exercise choices about professional health career paths, including those of clinical practice, teaching, and research. The committee also sees the need to create a more inclusive academic environment for math and science training, one that incorporates the understanding and appreciation of diversity as part of the effective teaching of these disciplines. The committee feels strongly that faculty members teaching science must be convinced that recruiting minority students to math and science, not weeding them out, is a major priority.

- *The committee urges a shift in perspective to an achievement model for minority education throughout the pipeline. To address current deficits, all educational institutions must set specific goals and implementation plans for inclusion and excellence.*

Only when significant value is placed on excellence and achievement, can effective strategies and programs be realized. A growing call for excellence should join with goals of racial diversity and access. As the face of America's population changes, it is no longer appropriate to define quality and excellence in education separate from the need to prepare students for the complex economic, social, educational, and cultural issues they will face in the world of work, family, and community. The importance of encouraging minorities to reach for lofty goals and giving them the confidence to achieve them cannot be overstated.

- *The committee advocates that reform agendas and change agents at all levels include an appreciation of cultural diversity, in ways that are guided by genuine respect for students' varying backgrounds, talents, and learning styles.*

All programs directed at broadening the educational pipeline must do a better job at reaching out to students, parents, and communities of all racial and ethnic groups. Schools need to mount specific efforts directed at creating and fostering attractive oases of learning and environments more conducive to granting respect—the real heart of multiculturalism and diversity.

- *The committee believes that the critical role of mentoring, with its proven track record of helping minorities pursue their aspirations and achieve their career goals, deserves to be more highly valued and to become a structured component of programs dedicated to a larger presence of minorities in the health professions.*

Minorities who have stayed the educational course often credit someone—a parent, a teacher, or mentor—for helping them to succeed. In assessing past efforts, the committee concluded that two critical components of successful programs are good teaching and mentoring, applied in a systematic way to students of all ages. Long-term mentoring commitments require a solid program infrastructure at the institutional level. In order not to place an undue mentoring burden on a few individuals within an institution, steps might be considered to develop a mentor-rich environment that will bring minority youths into open, trusting relationships with a variety of role models and supportive professionals.

- *The committee believes that educational institutions at all levels must promulgate the principle that "smart isn't something you are, it's something you can become."*

A growing body of literature shows that intellectual development is not dependent on special innate gifts, but is more the result of hard work and organized effort. The achievement gap in math and science is unlikely to diminish until, among other things, there are marked changes in the attitudes and beliefs of parents and students about education and the contribution of hard work and effort to academic success.

- *The committee advocates that diversity become prized as a resource, one characterized by genuine respect for students' varying backgrounds, talents, and learning styles.*

Diversity should be seen as a resource, as a criterion for excellence as our nation moves to a new stage of economic and scientific development. All programs directed at broadening the educational pathway must do better in reaching out to students, parents, and communities of all racial and ethnic groups. Encouraging minorities to pursue more advanced study in the sciences will require improving the climate of the classroom. All students must be made to feel that they are truly valued and that they can achieve academic success. This includes valuing their culture and language, and appreciating their individual talents.

- *A national priority must be the collection of better data and tracking systems to measure progress, to identify the most promising and effective interventions, as well as to identify those that are not working.*

Major obstacles can be eliminated by expanding or replicating existing successful intervention models. Yet, the committee found that only a few programs have been rigorously assessed or publicly evaluated. Nationwide there are successful programs, but many are overlooked as a result of lack of documentation and publication. There needs to be increasing emphasis on timely dissemination of evaluation findings in a format that can be used by all the various constituencies involved in these efforts.

- *The committee suggests that federal funding increasingly reflect the importance of supporting programs that improve the size and quality of the minority applicant pool by focusing on earlier interventions.*

A cohesive, strategic framework for broadening the pipeline for minorities in the health professions can make more effective use of existing resources.

Nevertheless, the administration's stated objective of developing a more diverse health professions workforce as a key component of health care reform and broadening access will require additional, well-targeted public resources. Federal funds must continue to be made available to those schools with demonstrated excellence in educating minority students. Incentives and rewards also should be directed at those academic health science centers willing to develop concerted efforts to increase the ranks of minority students and faculty.

- *The availability of good student financial assistance must be ensured through public and private sector scholarships.*

The high cost of medical education may be a critical factor constraining the size of the minority applicant pool and may make the quicker financial rewards of other career paths more attractive. Outstanding debt for indebted medical school graduates has grown significantly over the past 15 years, the result of major tuition increases and a decline in the availability of scholarships. To the extent that debt is an economic and psychological burden, medical schools may be in the paradoxical position of increasing constraints on the very students they seek to help.

- *Resources should be directed at faculty development, curricular revision, and program support for success in achieving greater minority participation at the university level.*

Successful strategies on the academic level require faculty time, initiative, innovation, and leadership. They require resources for faculty development, curricular revision, and program support, as well as meaningful incentives for faculty who participate. While universities, as well as other educational institutions, can appeal to the humanitarian impulses of faculty by asking them to be more alert for opportunities to improve the academic climate for minority students and faculty, the committee feels that appeals to altruistic values work best when they are accompanied by rewards and sanctions.

- *The committee believes that health care reform should recognize and promote opportunities for greater minority participation in the health professions and for better health service to minority populations.*

Developing a new research and action agenda for enhancing minority participation in the health professions is closely related to some of the most desired goals of health care reform: equity, justice, and greater economic productivity. The degree to which these goals are not now being achieved is apparent through the continued, striking differences between certain minority and majority groups for all of the key health status indicators. Increased diversity of health professionals has the potential for leading to better and more efficient patient care for minorities. Timely access and strong patient-provider relationships may lower health care costs through improving patient compliance, decreasing emergency room episodes, and reinforcing behavioral and lifestyle changes that reduce or eliminate risk factors, such as smoking or hypertension.

- *The committee also sees an urgent need to attract minority physicians to academic medicine and research.*

The career pathways of practitioners, researchers, and teachers are essential components; they should not be in competition with each other. Underrepresentation in the health professions is even more disturbing when one looks at the paltry number of minority faculty members in medical schools. The presence of a minority faculty member in a leadership position provides the atmosphere conducive to the recruitment, development, and retention of minority staff and faculty.

Minority students should be exposed to meaningful research experiences early in their academic careers, as early as at the high school level. Such an exposure could broaden the pool of individuals potentially interested in research and teaching positions, as well as contribute to success in the health professions. Minority researchers can contribute significantly to the need for enhanced study of the special conditions that contribute to poor health among minorities.

Recommendations

Through the contributions of the workshop participants, the committee developed six recommendations it feels, if followed, will lead to a strategic action and research agenda for increasing minority participation in the health professions.

- **The committee recommends that foundations, through a number of demonstration projects, sponsor communities that develop their own comprehensive plan for systematic reform and implement a dynamic, multifaceted community effort directed at minority health professions training, together with a goals statement and implementation plan.**

The formal education system alone cannot improve the problem of persistent minority underrepresentation. Future efforts will require a higher level of support among parents and all community-based leaders and organizations that contribute to education, health careers, mentoring, and the promotion of cultural diversity. Each community must become a place where learning can happen, a place that produces children equipped to make a wide array of choices and to succeed in the choices they make.

The committee envisions community efforts that involve institutions of learning from elementary schools through graduate training, churches, business leaders, health care organizations and providers, and other relevant stakeholders. The expectation is that such community-based efforts will raise the quality and environment for science teaching, attract additional resources, and make the prospect of a health or science career a stimulating, rewarding, and feasible career pathway. A significant component of the community initiative would be a structured grass-roots mentoring program, using the economic, financial, and social leverage of minority and nonminority individuals who have achieved professional standing in their neighborhoods. The committee believes that this kind of coordinated effort can bring about lasting changes in the attitude and behavior of the community.

- **The committee recommends that a national information network and clearinghouse be developed that provides timely information on activities relevant to minority health professionals.**

The committee believes that such a network would prove invaluable to students, faculty, and administrators. The use of electronic media and interactive communications to disseminate the latest data about educational opportunities, special programs, and financial aid would contribute significantly to broadening the interest and information base in this area. The availability of such a network should be widely advertised. Students, faculty, and mentors should be encouraged not only to use it but also to contribute to ongoing exchange of information.

- **The committee recommends that the federal government, the foundation world, and the private sector support an annual workshop and ongoing activities devoted to furthering the state of the art of mentoring in the health professions.**

Mentoring has proved to be a critical component of successful voyages through the health professions educational pipeline. Numerous mentoring organizations now exist, many of them engaged in efforts that have met with considerable success. However, more often than not, these kinds of activities are thinly funded. Much could be gained from providing an enrichment opportunity for individuals seriously engaged in mentoring to meet and learn from those who have developed especially effective programs.

- **The committee recommends that academic health centers set a higher priority toward enhanced minority participation and maintain a high level of sustained commitment to this goal. The committee encourages academic health centers to forge partnerships with major corporations and other educational entities targeted to building programs to attract and support youths interested in the health professions.**

Over the years, many of the nation's academic health centers and the Association of Academic Medical Colleges (AAMC) have made impressive contributions to advancing minorities in the health careers. Despite these worthy efforts, however, little evidence suggests that most medical schools have developed significant priorities and strategies to increase minority enrollment and faculty development. Many programs have been established as "additions" to ongoing efforts, but they have never become a part of the central, sustained mission of these institutions.

If the leadership of a medical school decides to make minority enrollment and faculty development a top priority, that school is likely to improve its record in this area. Instituting meaningful incentives and sanctions to promote desired outcomes, assigning staff time, and appointing a high-level administrator to address the issue are signs that institutions are serious about enhancing the presence of minorities in the nation's health care enterprise.

- **The committee recommends that community service and outreach become a fourth component of an academic health center's mission, in addition to teaching, research, and patient care. Similarly, the committee joins others in recommending formal inclusion of some level of community service among the criteria for academic recognition and advancement, in addition to the time-honored measures of scholarly and clinical achievement.**

Academic health centers increasingly need to form community partnerships with local schools and colleges to nurture the interest and to develop the talents of students who may have an interest in health careers. This partnership includes the need to study health and illness in the community setting. Faculty leading and joining such efforts often gain little recognition from the traditional academic reward systems. Implementing the committee recommendations would rapidly bring to academe a new sense of priority for community-based initiatives.

- **The committee calls on the corporate sector to develop and support multimedia campaigns to attract youngsters into the health professions. The committee suggests that relevant regulatory organizations within the communications industry be asked to establish a time bank, into which a defined percentage of all radio and TV time periods be deposited. Its objective would be to reserve a portion of America's public voice for social priorities.**

The imperative to enhance diversity in the health professions needs a more public voice. The media and their leaders have a key role to play in creating a critical mass of support for turning minority youth "on" to science and careers in medicine. Many educators have observed that children are born scientists, endlessly questioning where things come from and how they work. The media and those who develop advertising campaigns can help educate minority youth about the fun, prestige, challenge, and rewards, both financial and emotional, associated with careers in science and medicine.

1

Introduction

Greater and better use of the diverse human resources of our country is a national imperative. The underrepresentation of minorities in the health professions is but one indicator that we have failed to recognize and develop fully the human resources of our diverse population. Our ability to maintain a position of global leadership depends on our willingness to recognize, stimulate, and develop the capacities of all segments of society and to acknowledge the needs of those segments currently underrepresented in health careers. Policymakers have expressed concern about future productivity across most U.S. industries, including health, unless we can adopt policies that support the development of human resources within our diverse ethnic populations (Quality Education Project, 1990; Gore, 1993).

Past arguments for this kind of national call were based on a moral imperative for social equality and justice, but these arguments have sometimes proved inadequate to sustain the momentum for creating social change in institutions that provide opportunities directly or serve as channels to education and employment. The values of equity and fairness contributed to some positive changes in behavior and attitudes in earlier decades that increased the participation of minorities in the health professions (Simpson and Aronoff, 1988; Petersdorf et al., 1990; Ginzberg and Ostow, 1992). Those values still provide guidance and motivation, but it is now clear there are great benefits to the entire population from a commitment to diversity.

BACKGROUND

Minorities have long been underrepresented in the health professions, but it was not until the Civil Rights movement in the 1960s that particular attention was focused on this issue. When discussion around racial and ethnic distributions takes place, it is generally recognized that white is designated as majority and all other racial and ethnic groups are minority. Using the population parity model, African Americans, Native Americans, Mexican Americans, and mainland Puerto Ricans are underrepresented in the health professions. Within each racial or ethnic subcategory, significant differences can be found.*

After more than 20 years of programmatic activity there have been significant increases in minority enrollment. However, the proportion of minorities in all of the health professions schools is still lower than the representation of those groups in the population at large (Bureau of the Health Professions, 1993). During the mid-1970s, the number of persons applying to health professions schools reached a peak, followed by a decline. In the past few years, the numbers have increased again. Thus, when data are examined over a period of time, a notable increase in the numbers of minorities in the health professions is seen, although not in proportion to minority representation in the U.S. population. For example, in 1992, the number of minorities entering medical school was 1,827 (11.2 percent), the highest ever. Overall, 1992 medical school enrollment was 6,787 (10.3 percent), also the highest in many years. That same year the total number of underrepresented minority faculty increased from 2,082 (3.1 percent) in 1991 to 2,489 (3.5 percent) (AAMC [Association of American Medical Colleges], 1993a).

In looking at minority participation in the other health professions, medicine had the highest relative enrollment followed by dentistry, podiatry, and nursing. Osteopathy, optometry, and veterinary medicine had the lowest relative minority enrollment. Pharmacy was in the middle of the two extremes (Ready and Nickens, forthcoming).

Compelling demographic trends alone speak to the value and wisdom of broadening educational opportunities for minorities to pursue careers in medicine as well as other professional callings that contribute so much to a nation's strength and productivity. In the 1950s, nearly 9 of every 10 Americans were of European descent. Today, 1 of every 4 adults and 1 of every 3 children are of African, Latin American, or Asian origin. Minorities are increasing faster than the rest of the population. Indeed, the Bureau of the Census predicts that by the year 2000, minorities, who today are one-fifth of the national population, will have accounted for 60 percent of the total population growth (Action

---

*There has been increasing pressure from racial and ethnic groups not presently included as "underrepresented minorities" to achieve recognition. Thus, as a result of the changing racial and ethnic composition of the U.S. population, there are increasing calls to include other groups within this definition of underrepresented, potentially modifying the historically monitored trends.

INTRODUCTION

Council on Minority Education, 1990). Such trends are enough reason to reenergize the agenda for more equitable representation of minorities in health careers.

In recent years, however, mounting social and political pressures calling for major reform of the nation's health care system added yet another dimension of timeliness and urgency to the issue of enhanced minority representation in clinical practice and teaching. As part of his health care reform plan, President Clinton has articulated the importance of developing a medical workforce to better reflect the nation's present and future health care needs. As this country embarks on a historical national dialogue for restructuring the health care system, the goal of making health care more appropriate, affordable, and accessible for all our citizens will be receiving priority attention.

These new and powerful dynamics stimulated the Institute of Medicine (IOM), with its long interest and commitment to improving the quality and context of our health care system, to appoint a committee that would assess strategies that have focused on helping minority students attain their health career goals. Its findings would assist in developing an action and research agenda responsive to our nation's social and economic needs.

The IOM Committee on Increasing Minority Participation in the Health Professions was asked to develop a future-oriented research and strategic action agenda for increasing the participation of minorities in the health professions. Two tasks framed the committee's charge:

- consider the multiple aspects of professional development, such as education, academic achievement, opportunity, and mentoring, that affect participation of underrepresented minorities in the health professions; and
- address the field of health professions from a global, broadly defined perspective, with a more targeted focus on minority participation in clinical practice and academic medicine.

The committee's deliberations were enhanced through the information it received from three commissioned papers and the informed and spirited deliberations of participants in the workshop it convened. Appendix A provides the authors and titles of the papers and a roster of workshop attendees.

The committee discussed a future health professions workforce that looks more like America, where clinicians, researchers, and teachers increasingly reflect the cultural and ethnic diversity that has contributed so much to our nation and holds the key to its future. Although ethnic minorities are expected to continue to grow significantly for the next several decades, they remain vastly underrepresented in clinical practice, teaching, and health sciences research.

The committee's concerns are not new. For more than 25 years, many individuals and institutions have shared a common goal of increasing the participation of minorities in all aspects of health care. As Chapters 2 and 3 indicate, many resources have been directed toward realizing this goal. Today we appear to be embarking on a new period of concentration and energy to address this issue, spurred by disturbing reports of persistent and, in some cases, growing disparities in access between underrepresented minorities and whites, the reality of America's demographic revolution, and the declining status of the United States in the global economy.

In its review of the programmatic interventions discussed in Chapter 3, the committee found that both the public and the private sectors have supported many laudable efforts to enhance the pipeline for minority training in the health professions. Viewed from a national perspective, however, these achievements have not built the institutional and academic infrastructure necessary to eliminate the gap between vision and reality. In an environment of demographic changes and major reforms in health care and in education, the nation cannot afford to fail in generating valid opportunities for minorities to significantly contribute to its social and economic productivity. Minorities, if given the opportunity to participate effectively in the health professions, can contribute to a more equitable and productive society, and help the United States maintain a position of economic and moral leadership in the world.

The vision of a more diverse and democratic society is an essential feature of the American dream for the twenty-first century. The committee believes that both the recruitment and the retention of greater numbers of African Americans, Hispanics, and Native Americans represent a critical cog in moving the vision to reality.

SIGNIFICANCE OF THE PROBLEM

Several national developments point to the importance of having a better understanding of how to improve the recruitment and retention of minorities in the health professions. This problem does not exist in a vacuum.

The increasing diversity of the U.S. population is creating new challenges to our democracy. By the year 2000, African Americans, Hispanics, and Native Americans will constitute almost one-fourth of the U.S. population (COGME [Council on Graduate Medical Education], 1992). Some cities even now reflect some of the growing tensions related to demographic change. Urban riots in Los Angeles, Miami, Atlanta, New York, and other cities provide a "glimpse of the agony and the anger, the struggle and the success of a diverse but still distinct wedge of the population" (Stanfield, 1992). The 1992 Los Angeles eruption, in particular, was but one stark indication that, in spite of some advances, much remains to be done to overcome the problems of poverty, discrimination, and alienation experienced by minority communities.

The committee did not try to address these major problems, a task that was beyond its ability and charge, but it considered the background of demographic change that characterizes this period of our history. The committee approached the study from the perspective of enriching the current and future ethnic mix of health professionals rather than increasing overall numbers. In its call for greater participation, this report reflects several other developments in the United States that are discussed below.

Need to Improve Health Services for Minorities

Ethnicity is a very important element in determining and evaluating morbidity and mortality. But socioeconomic status is also very significant: How people live, get sick, and die depends not only on their ethnicity, but also on their socioeconomic condition. The quality of health of any individual or any nation is the result of not only having access to adequate health care services, but also having adequate education, income, and housing (Reed et al., 1992; Angell, 1993; Pappas et al., 1993).

The increasing diversity of our population has been accompanied by persistent gaps in health status, with certain populations disproportionately affected by some of the most debilitating diseases of our time, including heart disease, cancer, diabetes mellitus, and HIV/AIDS (U.S. Department of Health and Human Services, 1985). Trauma, the fourth most costly disease in the U.S., disproportionately affects underrepresented minorities (Munoz et al., 1992). Over the course of the twentieth century, African Americans have made substantial progress in life expectancy, with the gap between whites and African Americans narrowing from 15 years at the beginning of the century to less than 7 years currently (National Center for Health Statistics, 1992). However, a substantial difference in life expectancy remains, and in recent years, this gap is again widening, due in part to drug use, HIV infection, and homicide, as well as lack of access to adequate health care. While the infant mortality rate has decreased for both the African-American and the white populations, the rate for African Americans is still twice as high as that for whites. Hispanics continue to have a much higher incidence of Type II (adult onset) diabetes, approximately two to three times that of the non-Hispanic population.

The literature on access to care provides extensive evidence that Americans of racial and ethnic minorities use fewer health care services than nonminorities, despite having a greater need for care. Even when there is entry into the health care system, minorities receive less aggressive medical care (Whittle et al., 1993). Being of a racial or ethnic minority is highly correlated with underuse and less appropriate use of health care services as well as with worse outcomes. Compared to whites, African Americans and Hispanics have fewer doctors' visits, are more likely to use the hospital emergency department or outpatient clinics as their regular source of care, and have higher rates of morbidity and mortality from preventable diseases (Institute of Medicine, 1988, 1990; Billings and Teicholz, 1990). Efforts to understand the reasons for these disparities have been hampered by data limitations.

The Council on Ethical and Judicial Affairs of the American Medical Association (AMA) has concluded that persistent, and sometimes substantial, differences continue to exist between the health status of African Americans and their white counterparts. The council emphasizes the need for greater access to health care for African Americans and for greater awareness among physicians of existing and potential disparities in treatment (AMA Council on Ethical and Judicial Affairs, 1990). Similar findings were reported by the AMA's Council on Scientific Affairs in its 1991 report on Hispanic health in the United States. In an issue of the *Journal of the American Medical Association* devoted to this topic, the council points out that Hispanics are the fastest growing minority group in the United States; Hispanic subgroups need to be considered separately; and poverty, lack of insurance, and level of acculturation are the greatest impediments to health care for this population (AMA Council on Scientific Affairs, 1991).

While a host of factors—socioeconomic, genetic, cultural, and institutional—determine an individual's health status and use of health care services, a starting point to improving minority access may be to increase the supply of minority physicians. Although the link between improved access and the number of minority health providers is weak, the literature suggests that interactions between provider and patient race, ethnicity, and gender affect access to and use of health care services (COGME, 1992).

Data and information do illustrate that minority physicians show a greater tendency to practice in their communities or other underserved areas. In 1988, 48.9 percent of minority medical school graduates said they planned to practice in socioeconomically deprived areas, while only 13.6 percent of their nonminority peers reported such plans. In 1993, figures for both groups dropped, with 36 percent of minority students still preparing to serve in deprived areas while the percentage for all graduates fell to 8 percent (AAMC, 1993a). Further, some evidence links the quality of health care with accessibility to and use of primary care physicians. Minority physicians, either by choice or by necessity, tend to practice as primary care physicians (COGME, 1992; Hopkins, 1992; Fox, 1993).

After extensive discussions as well as reviews of commissioned papers on various aspects of this topic, the committee believes that an increase in the participation of minorities in the structures and processes used to determine research priorities, research protocols, and health services delivery will provide new opportunities to broaden our understanding of the science and art of effective health care, not only for minorities but for the public in general.

Professional Development for All Personnel

Minorities practicing medicine, teaching classes, and conducting research in a joint endeavor with other health professionals can lead to more empathetic communication and health care for minority patients and patients in general. According to recent statistics from the National Science Foundation, about 11,500 African-American, Hispanic, Asian, and Native American researchers work in the life sciences, compared with 104,300 whites. In addition:

- African Americans constitute 10.1 percent of the workforce, but only 3.7 percent of the nation's physicians, only 2.1 percent of the nation's dentists, and only 2.4 percent of the nation's natural scientists.
- Hispanics make up 6.9 percent of the total workforce, yet only 5.5 percent of the nation's physicians, 3.3 percent of the nation's dentists, and 2.7 percent of the nation's natural scientists.
- Of the 4,779 doctorates awarded in the life sciences in this country in 1990, only eight went to Native Americans (Healy, 1992).

While there are important roles to be played by other professionals and disciplines in the movement toward a more inclusive and comprehensive agenda for health, this study targets those institutions and professionals most directly responsible for developing the strategies and programs for training the future health workforce. Recent research findings suggest that sectors other than the health care sector must contribute to reducing the disparities of health status in minorities. But it is principally the responsibility of the health care professional to translate relevant social, fiscal, and scientific developments and apply them to effective health care (Ginzberg and Ostow, 1991; Dougherty, 1992).

Loss in Economic Productivity

The net loss to the U.S. economy resulting from the disproportionately poor health status of minority populations is difficult to measure accurately. Nevertheless, most analysts would argue that a healthy workforce is more productive than one that is less healthy. Minority health care providers are more likely to be culturally sensitive to their populations and to organize the delivery system in ways that better suit their health care needs (COGME, 1992). Increased diversity of health professionals has the potential for leading to better and more efficient patient care for minorities. Timely access and strong patient-provider relationships may diminish health care costs through improving patient compliance, decreasing emergency room episodes, and reinforcing behavioral and lifestyle changes that reduce or eliminate risk factors, such as smoking (Edwards, forthcoming).

Influencing and Improving Public Policy

The issue of greater representation for minorities goes beyond increased access and better health care. Many of the researchers, analysts, and other leaders who frame health policies, develop priorities for allocating resources, and identify new interventions are drawn largely from the faculties of health professions schools. Minorities are severely underrepresented among these faculties and the consequences are considerable. In 1992, they made up only 3.5 percent of the faculty members in medical schools. If one removes traditional minority medical schools—Howard, Meharry, Morehouse, and the University of Puerto Rico—from these calculations, the minority faculty representation in the remaining 122 medical schools falls to approximately 2.6 percent (AAMC, 1993a). Unfortunately, internal medicine, the specialty that produces the majority of academicians in medicine, lags behind the overall percentage for minority faculty at medical schools at 2.9 percent. There also appears to be an especially disturbing lack of minorities in senior faculty positions particularly at the level of deans and senior academic officers in our health science institutions. Professional associations such as the Association of Academic Minority Physicians articulate these concerns at the national level.

Implicit in the paucity of representation is the message that faculty status and influence are not readily achievable goals or realistic professional options for minority students in medicine. The situation is similar for the other health professions as well (National Research Council, 1989). Thus, the absence of immediate access to educators who have shared their experiences can often constitute a significant void in the course of training for students who are struggling with questions about career choices and the odds of and obstacles to success.

Facilitating Institutional Change

An institution's commitment to increasing its opportunities for minorities is often influenced by the strong support of minority faculty, whose advocacy may range from subtle consciousness-raising to aggressive promotion of change. The need for more minority representation on admission and evaluation committees has been long apparent. This need has perhaps less to do with the lack of fairness in the process than with the acknowledgment of the importance of diversity among those who select and evaluate future professionals to serve the broad and heterogeneous needs of the population. Diversity at these levels ensures that the institution's intentions and commitment will be communicated to those persons it wishes to persuade toward careers such as medicine and health services research (Cregler et al., 1993; Ready and Nickens, 1993).

Community Leadership and Advocacy

Still another reason for the focus on increasing the participation of minorities relates to community leadership and advocacy. Health professionals, particularly physicians, represent not only respected professions, but also important sources of leadership for their local communities (Nickens, 1992; Cregler et al., 1993). They serve on boards and commissions and in other essential community leadership roles. As minority and majority health professionals work together as partners with community leaders, the community develops pride in its diversity. Through membership in and support of minority professional societies, such as the National Medical Association, National Black Nurses Association, or the National Dental Association, minorities can more effectively accomplish what they could not do individually. These societies can provide leadership in community efforts to enhance health and can improve educational opportunities for others who are aspiring to the professions.

Relevance to Health Care Reform

Developing a new research and action agenda for enhancing minority participation in the health professions is closely related to some of the most desired goals of health care reform: equity, justice, and greater economic productivity. The degree to which these goals are not now being achieved is apparent through the continued, striking differences between certain minority and majority groups for all of the key health status indicators.

An increasing acknowledgment of the primary care physician's importance in health care is emerging, and it is reflected in Medicare's new resource-based, relative value scale payment structure and in the pivotal role given to primary care in all of the major health care reform proposals. Higher percentages of young African-American and Hispanic physicians choose primary care specialties than either white or other young physicians (Cohen et al., 1990; Ginzberg et al., 1993). It is too early to tell what health care reform will mean to minorities in the health care professions, but every indication is that stronger incentives will be placed on developing a health professions workforce more responsive to the nation's changing demographic profile and its different health care needs (American Health Security Act, 1993; Gore, 1993).

Members of our society widely believe that a basic level of medical care should be available to all citizens. Little consensus exists, however, on how to finance universal access and what package of benefits should be assured. Nevertheless, as the debates on how to assure universal access to appropriate and necessary health care become more intense, it is important to ensure that the guardians of this public good mirror the country's cultural diversity.

Relevance to Reform in Public Education

A growing body of literature indicates that universal access to health care may do little to improve health status if public education and other essential social support systems are underdeveloped (Starfield, 1991; Pappas et al., 1993). The education of health professionals is strongly influenced by the quality of public education, which is in a period of great change. If the United States wants to compete as a first-class economy, it is imperative that it develop its human resources to much higher levels of skill and competence. Especially important will be developing the talents of minorities, who along with white women and immigrants, will constitute almost 90 percent of the new growth of our workforce for the rest of this century (Action Council on Minority Education, 1990).

Unlike the reform movement of the post-Sputnik era, which sought to increase the numbers of highly trained young people who were talented in science and engineering, the current focus is on "Science for Every American" (Ebert, 1993). Higher-quality schooling for everyone will make a difference in preparing more students for entry into professional and technical training. To avoid widening the existing gap, every effort is being made to broaden the base of competence in science and mathematics education in an inclusive manner. This approach could create more opportunities for minorities and eliminate some of the existing barriers to professional development.

Science and mathematics are important core subjects in preparing for the health professions, but the committee did not limit its attention to them. Its deliberations pointed to the belief that learning cannot take place effectively outside a context of racial diversity. Effective learning for today's social, economic, and intellectual challenges can take place only in environments that allow for understanding the total human experience. Quality education must now mean promoting interaction that allows people to see each other from their own cultural vantage points (Jennings, 1989). These interactive settings may result in the questioning and challenging of traditional economic, cultural, and political arrangements.

Before change can happen, the underlying issues and facts must be understood. The next chapter looks at what happens to students throughout their educational years and how it eventually affects minority participation in health professions.

2

Factors That Define the Pipeline

Major social forces and strong political leadership helped bring about the increases in minority enrollment in the health professions that began in 1968. At that time, the climate of the Civil Rights era and good economic times in the United States converged, and the nation seemed poised to commit itself to overcoming the barriers to full participation by minorities in the health professions (Epps et al., 1993).

The promise was not fulfilled, however. Progress in matriculating minorities came virtually to a halt in the mid-1970s, particularly in medicine, which had been at the forefront of efforts to educate minority students (AAMC, 1993a). Even with the recent upswing in applicants and new entrants, the proportion of minorities in all the health professions schools is still lower than the representation of these groups in the population at large.

No one can point to the sole reason for the persistent underrepresentation in minority enrollment and its subsequent impact on the number of minority health professionals in the United States. Some of the stalled progress in the late 1970s and through the 1980s has been attributed to a slower economy, a diminished domestic agenda, declining interest in providing educational opportunities to minorities, and the publication of the 1980 Medical Education National Advisory Committee report, which predicted a significant oversupply of physicians in most specialties by the year 2000. But minority students also report an insidious set of less tangible barriers—both academic and social—that have been strewn along their paths: denial of access to quality education; teachers who expect too little of students; anti-intellectual peer pressure; and a cultural gap between the world in which they study and that of their family and neighborhood (Epps et al., 1993; Ready and Nickens, 1993).

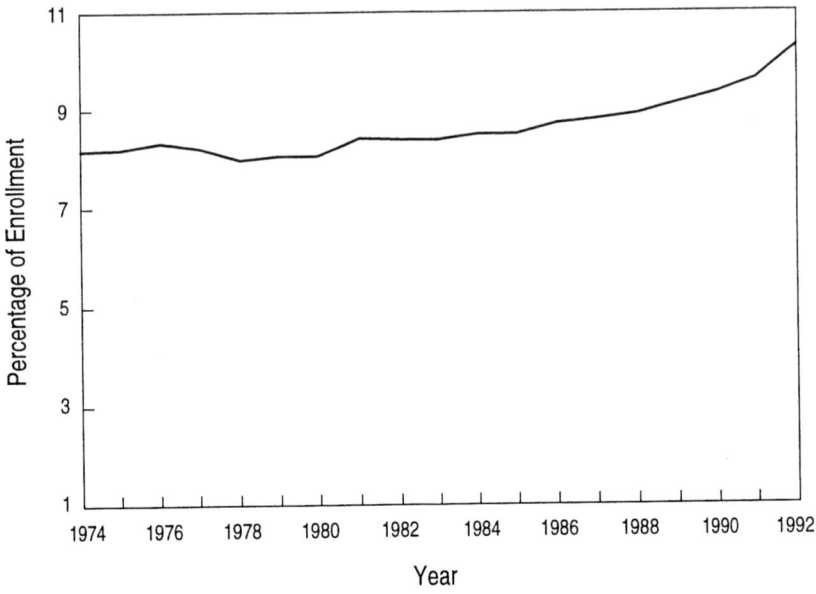

Figure 2-1. Underrepresented minorities as a percentage of total enrollment. SOURCE: Minority Students in Medical Education: Facts and Figures VII, AAMC, 1993.

This is not to say there have not been successes in the last 25 years. The nation's historically black colleges and universities, which once educated three-quarters of all African-American doctors (Odegaard, 1977), have continued to play an important role in producing minority physicians. A number of other institutions, particularly some medical schools, and organizations such as the National Medical Fellowships, Inc., the National Urban Coalition, the Association of American Medical Colleges (AAMC), the National Medical Association, and a number of private foundations have put significant resources into efforts to increase the number of underrepresented minorities in the health care professions and other science-intensive disciplines.

Figure 2-2 presents the colleges that provided the largest numbers of medical school matriculants in 1992. Such efforts alone, however, cannot overcome the disadvantages of an education obtained in the poorly funded and staffed schools that educate many minority students, or the lack of a concerted commitment by a broader spectrum of schools toward a larger minority presence (College Board, 1985; NRC [National Research Council], 1989).

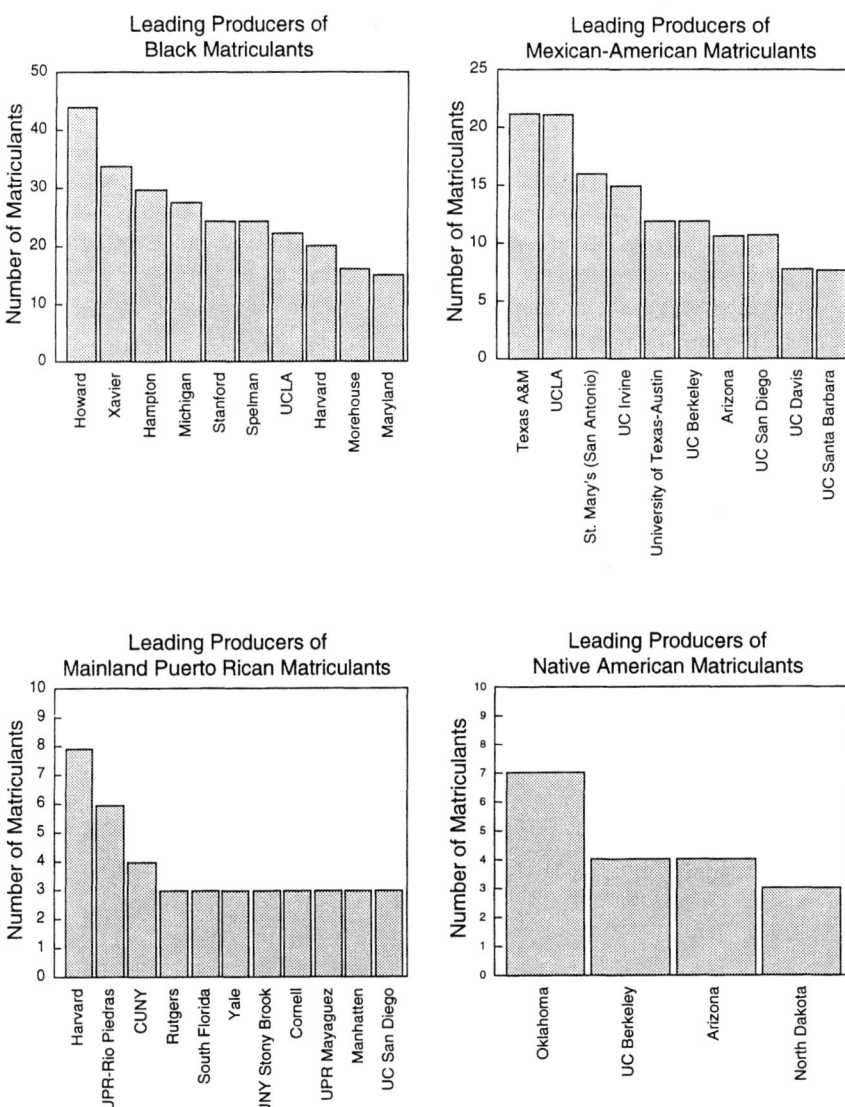

Figure 2-2. Leading college producers of underrepresented minority medical school matriculants, 1992. SOURCE: National Network for Health Science Partnerships News, AAMC, 1993.

Studies and other data tend to reinforce the notion that most minority students are not educated to the same level as their white counterparts (Action Council on Minority Education, 1990). And there is growing evidence that the failures of the students who slip off the various paths that lead to careers in the health professions must be shared by society and by the institutions responsible for educating young people (NRC, 1989). Among nonminority health professions schools, enrollment and performance statistics suggest that many institutions still have much to do to fully understand and address the problems confronting minority students. For example, minority students continue to be overrepresented among students repeating their first year of medical school or who do not complete their medical school training (AAMC, 1993a).

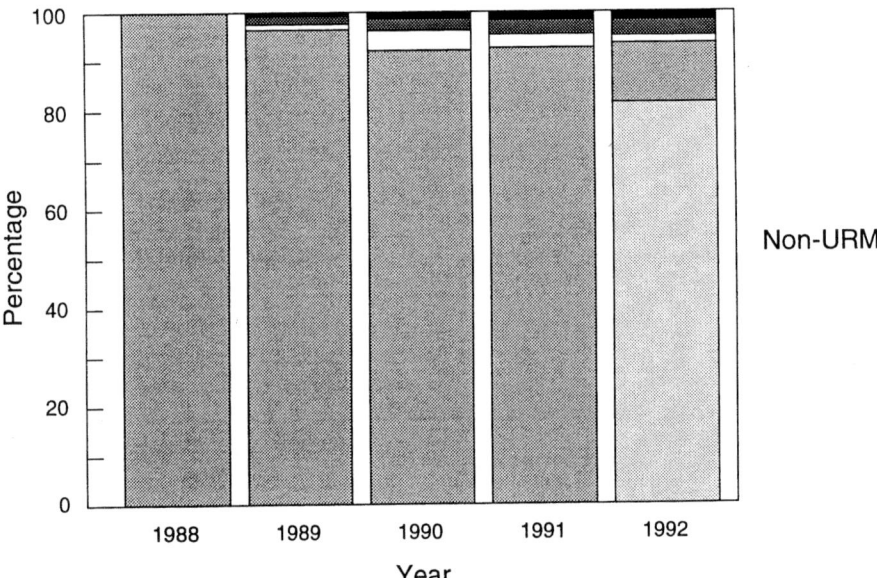

Figure 2-3a. Academic progression of 1988 non-URM matriculants. SOURCE: Minority Students in Medical Education: Facts and Figures VII, AAMC, 1993.

This chapter focuses on the pipeline beginning with the early school years when students first turn away, or are directed away, from careers in the health professions. It then presents information about the enrollment and fate of minority students entering medical and health professions schools and discusses the factors associated with minority underrepresentation.

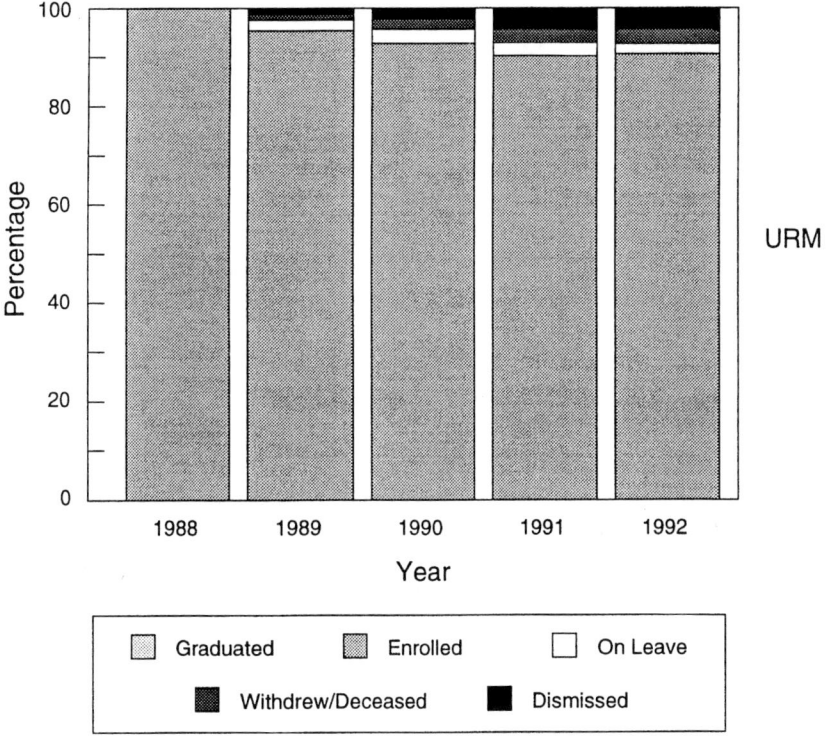

Figure 2-3b. Academic progression of 1988 URM matriculants. SOURCE: Same as Figure 2-3a.

African Americans, Hispanics, and Native Americans comprise about 20 percent of the U.S. population and 19 percent of its workforce, yet underrepresented minorities make up only 5 percent of the science and engineering workforce (U.S. Bureau of the Census, 1990; National Science Foundation [NSF], 1992). They have hardly fared better in the health professions. For example, little more than 8 percent of the nation's physicians and 11 percent of the nation's registered nurses are non-Asian minorities (U.S. Bureau of the Census, 1990).

WHERE THE LEAK BEGINS

The failure to stop the leaks in the pipeline starts early. Children begin their schooling with much curiosity about how the natural world works, but studies have shown that the school environment quickly erodes that interest (Gibbons, 1992a). Minorities start to fall behind in science and math by the fourth grade, and sometimes as early as second grade (Gibbons, 1992a). African-American students start school with test scores that fall within the same range as those of whites their age, but by the sixth grade, African Americans in many school districts are two full grade levels behind whites in achievement (Steele, 1992).

In recent years it has become clear that the quality and quantity of mathematical instruction given to students throughout their academic lives determine how prepared they will be for science-based careers. A study by the College Board, which administers the Scholastic Aptitude Test (SAT), found that high school students who took 1 or more years of algebra in high school were 2 to 3.5 times more likely to go to college than students who did not take algebra. Although white high school graduates are more likely to attend college than are African Americans, African-American students who studied algebra in high school are as likely to attend college as white students (Pelavin and Kane, 1990). According to the National Science Foundation, however, many minority students lack proper guidance and often enroll in algebra in 10th or 11th grade, too late to prepare them for college entrance exams (Selvin, 1992).

Numerous studies and surveys suggest a high degree of interest in science studies among high school students. But that interest does not seem to be exploited in a way that increases the numbers of students who go on to careers in the health professions (Mullis and Jenkins, 1988; NSF, 1992).

Figure 2-4 shows that an average of 86,000 minority students are interested in pursuing studies in the natural sciences and engineering in their sophomore year of high school. By the senior year of high school, that number has fallen to 65,000. In the freshman year of college, only 40,000 are still studying mathematics and science. This number falls to 14,000 by the junior year. Finally, 13,000 minority students earn B.S. degrees in science or engineering, 2,500 enter graduate studies, and 2,000 earn M.S. degrees (NSF, 1992). Difficult and impersonal introductory science courses are often cited as the specific reason many high school and beginning college students leak out of the medical school pipeline (Petersdorf, 1991).

Even as the number of students attending college increased in the 1980s, African Americans, Hispanics, and Native Americans continued to be underrepresented (NRC, 1989; Carter and Wilson, 1993). According to a recent American Council on Education report, whites are far more likely to participate in higher education than African Americans or Hispanics. In 1991, for example, of white 18- to 24-year-olds, 34.1 percent were in college, compared with 18 percent of Hispanics in that age group and 23.6 percent of all African Americans in that age group (U.S. Department of Education, 1991; Carter and Wilson, 1992). Underrepresented minorities showed a 9.1 percent enrollment gain from 1990 to 1991, most of it at 2-year institutions (U.S. Department of Education, 1991). However, college participation rates, which show how many students in the 18- to 24-year-old range have "ever enrolled in college," declined for African Americans from 48 percent in 1990 to 46.1 percent in 1991, while the percentage of Hispanics increased 3 percentage points to 47.6 percent (U.S. Department of Education, 1991). Schools in some states recruited greater numbers and percentages of minority students at 2- and 4-year institutions, but in fact, enrollment gains lagged far behind actual population increases for some ethnic minorities (Carter and Wilson, 1993). The American Council on Education report on the status of minorities in higher education cited a study that estimated the disparities would grow in the coming decade (Carter and Wilson, 1993). By 1995, according to projections from 22 states, the number of African-American public high school graduates will drop, creating another potential barrier to progress for this group and its representation in college (Western Interstate Commission for Higher Education and the College Board, 1991).

It is clear that in addition to learning what steps to take to retain students in courses of study that lead to the health professions, educators and policymakers must consider how to increase the number of students who take those courses, as well as the number of teachers who encourage them to do so. Statistics show that students of all races become too discouraged, or fail to receive the encouragement they need, to continue their studies in the sciences and engineering. Only a fraction of interested high school students—1.4 percent—go on to earn Ph.D. degrees. Only 0.4 percent of minority students emerge with Ph.D. degrees in science and engineering (NSF, 1992). It is from this small group that the health professions schools draw, and compete, for their applicants.

Studies indicate that most of the qualified minority students in this country are already applying to medical school. In 1990, there were 2,709 African Americans, 1,637 Hispanics, and 207 Native Americans awarded bachelor's degrees in the life sciences and physical sciences in the United States. Among students applying to medical school that year, 2,349 were African American, 1,338 were Hispanic, and 132 were Native American (Ready and Nickens, 1993). It is clear from these numbers that medical schools are attracting almost all the nation's Hispanic and African-American science graduates. This finding suggests that more intensive recruiting efforts among science graduates would not significantly increase the number of minority applicants, and that there may be a dearth of minority science graduates to enter other science-based careers (Ready and Nickens, 1993; Ready and Nickens, forthcoming).

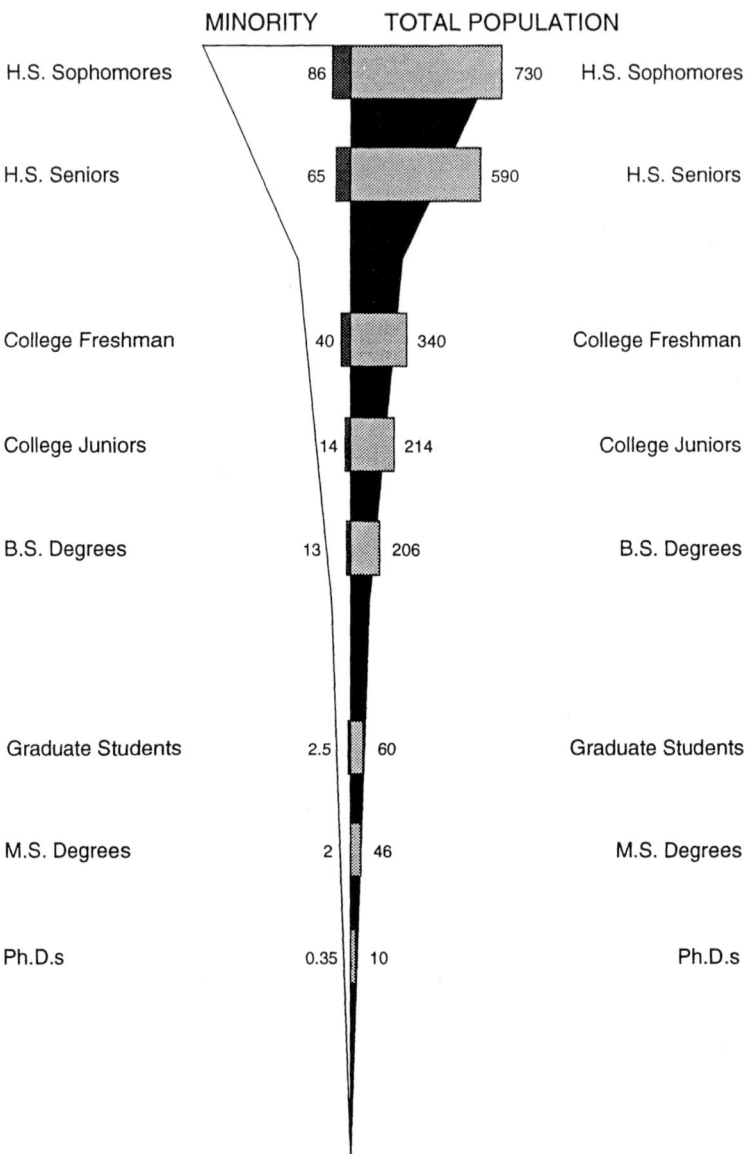

Figure 2-4. Natural sciences and engineering pipeline (thousands of students). SOURCE: Science 258:1178, November 13, 1992. Copyright by the American Association for the Advancement of Science. Reprinted with permission.

Medical School

With the exception of the historically black medical schools, most medical schools began recruiting minority students during the late 1960s and early 1970s. Until the mid-1960s, medical schools such as Meharry College School of Medicine and Howard University College of Medicine educated three-quarters of the nation's African-American physicians (Odegaard, 1977).

Many of the early gains in admissions came with the establishment of new medical schools and the expansion of class size in other schools. Student ferment, the rise of Dr. Martin Luther King, Jr., and the riots that followed his assassination also played a powerful role in nudging policymakers and educators toward establishing new reinforcement and enrichment programs together with scholarship money to help minority students obtain medical degrees. Many of these positive endeavors were made possible through federal funding sponsored by the Health Careers Opportunity Program (HCOP) of the Division of Disadvantaged Assistance, Bureau of Health Professions. since 1972, HCOP has been dedicated to increasing the number of minority disadvantaged individuals in health careers. By 1972, according to one survey, most medical schools had initiated programs to increase minority enrollment: two-thirds of the surveyed schools had altered admissions procedures and three-fourths had altered their admissions criteria (Epps et al., 1993). These factors pushed the first-year enrollment of underrepresented minorities from 4 percent in 1970 to 10 percent in 1974 (Petersdorf, 1991).

In the 15 years that followed, however, there was little change in the percentage of minority students enrolled in medical schools (Figure 2-5). Among the reasons was a declining interest in using affirmative action to right past wrongs (Epps et al., 1993; Ready and Nickens, 1993). Speaking in 1991, Robert Petersdorf, president of the Association of American Medical Colleges, observed, "The chances for an underrepresented student to be admitted to medical school have actually become more remote as their proportion of the total U.S. population continues to rise" (Petersdorf, 1991).

In its most recent data release, the AAMC reports that the number of minority medical school matriculants reached 1,827, or 11.2 percent, the highest ever (AAMC, 1993a). This parallels an upsurge in overall applications to medical school. The total enrollment of minorities in medical school was 6,787, or 10.3 percent, also the highest in many years (AAMC, 1993a).

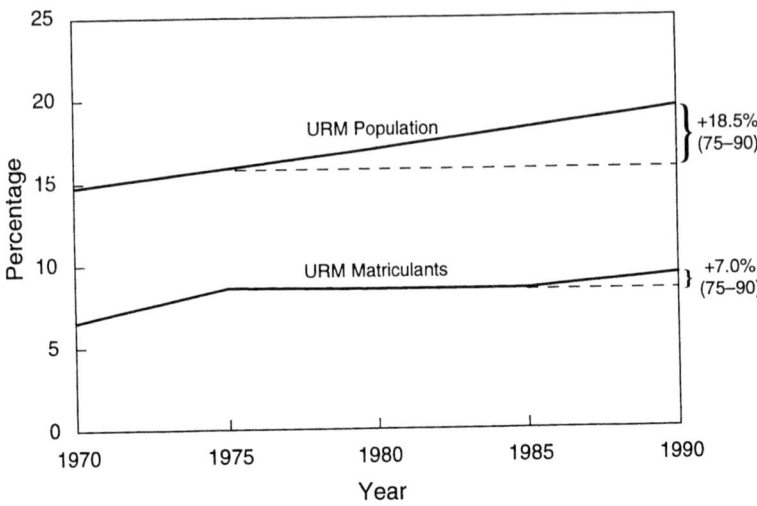

Figure 2-5. Underrepresented minorities as a percentage of the U.S. population and medical school matriculants: 1970-1990. SOURCE: Ready, T.P., and Nickens, H.W. Inventory and Analysis of the Effectiveness of Strategies and Programs for Increasing Minority Participation in Medicine. Paper prepared for the Institute of Medicine's Study to Increase Minority Participation in the Health Professions, 1993.

In its report, the AAMC describes the average 1992 underrepresented minority medical school matriculant as female; from a family in which the parents are either professionals or in sales, with some post-high school education, and earning a combined income of $56,661 (AAMC, 1993a). Women were 57 percent of underrepresented applicants, compared to 42 percent among all applicants. This profile indicates that the pool of applicants may be limited to an elite spectrum of the minority population, particularly in terms of education and income. The AAMC report supports the finding that post-high school education among parents is one of the few consistent predictors of whether a student goes to medical school, providing more reason for raising the educational level of all minority students (Robert Wood Johnson Foundation, 1987; AAMC, 1993a).

The Admissions Process

The use of quantitative measures, such as the Medical College Admissions Test (MCAT) and grade point averages (GPAs), cannot predict or guarantee a student's success in medical school. Although many schools have not studied this matter, most medical school admissions officers have a sense of what combination of MCAT scores and GPAs in college is required to minimize the risk of academic failure. In a 1987 study, admissions officers were asked what score on the 15-point MCAT they would find acceptable in an applicant to medical school. Eleven was cited as the mean exemplary score; seven was the mean acceptable score. Some admissions officers found four an acceptable score; others would not accept less than ten (Mitchell, 1987).

Medical school admissions committees, under a mandate to increase the percentage of minority students, admit underrepresented minorities with lower MCAT scores and GPAs than their white counterparts. These scores have improved in recent years, particularly among African Americans, but African Americans are still being accepted at much lower rates than whites (Ready and Nickens, 1993). No studies have been done to explain this disparity, or to explain why minority medical students continue to repeat the first year of medical school far more often than do white students. Of the 790 students who repeated their first year of medical school or were taking a decelerated course load in the 1992–1993 school year, for example, 294 were underrepresented minorities (AAMC, 1993a).

In comparison to other medical students, underrepresented minorities are somewhat less likely to complete medical school, although their chances of doing so are improving. Surveys conducted by the AAMC show that by the fourth year of medical school, for the entering class of 1988, the percentage of underrepresented minorities retained was 92.2 percent, compared to 96.4 for all students (AAMC, 1993a).

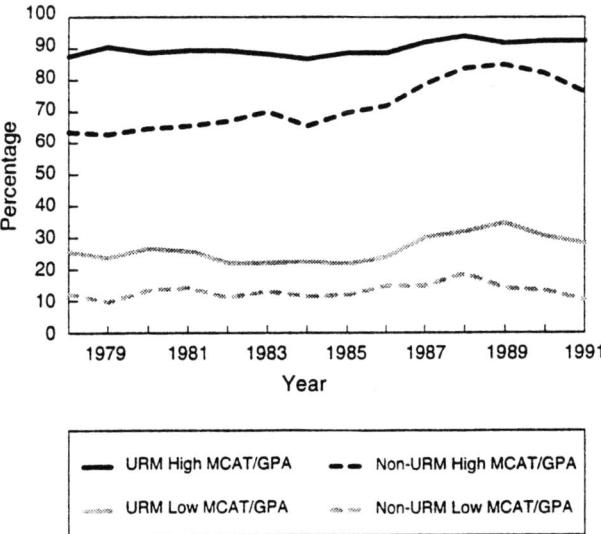

Figure 2-6. Acceptance rates by MCAT and GPA for underrepresented minorities and all other applicants, 1978–1991. SOURCE: Minority Students in Medical Education: Facts and Figures VII, AAMC, 1993.

It has been argued that medical schools could solve the problem of underrepresentation if they accepted all or most of the underrepresented minorities who applied to medical school, and if the institutions took whatever steps necessary to produce board-certified physicians (Ready and Nickens, 1993). To implement such a strategy, medical schools would have to provide expensive programs of academic support and would have to allow students to spend 5 or 6 years in medical school. For a number of reasons, including political considerations, such a strategy is unlikely to be pursued by medical schools (Ready and Nickens, 1993).

Other Health Professions Schools

The best reported data on minorities entering the health professions come from the field of medicine. Comparable data for other specialties are difficult to obtain. Definitive racial and ethnic categories have not been universally established or accepted, and professional associations have adopted and adapted classifications to correspond to their needs and ability to ascertain racial and ethnic identity.

Nevertheless, since 1974, the U.S. Department of Health and Human Services' Bureau of Health Professions has published *Minorities and Women in the Health Fields*, which provides data on the representation of minorities and women in health occupations and in education programs leading to health careers. Data from the most recent edition, published in 1990, and additional data from the 1991–1992 academic year provided by the Bureau show some modest upward trends in the proportional representation in first-year and total enrollment across the other professions, but these increases remain well below population parity (Tables 2-1 and 2-2).

In 1991–1992, the latest year for which the Bureau of Health Professions has comprehensive data, the racial and ethnic minority representation in first-year classes of health professions schools ranges from lows of 5.8 percent for veterinary medicine and 7.1 percent for osteopathic medicine, to highs of 17.8 percent for podiatry, 13.5 percent for all types of registered nursing programs, and 12.5 percent for dentistry (HRSA [Health Resources and Services Administration], personal communication, 1993).

In terms of total enrollment, minorities remain least well represented in veterinary medicine (6.9 percent) and osteopathic medicine (7.8 percent), while best represented in podiatric medicine (17.9 percent), dentistry (13.4 percent), and allopathic medicine (10.3 percent).

Table 2-1. Underrepresented Minorities (African Americans, Hispanics, Native Americans): Representation in U.S. Population and in 1st year classes (selected health professions), 1971–1992.

	'70–'71	'71–'72	'72–'73	'73–'74	'74–'75	'75–'76	'76–'77	'77–'78	'78–'79	'79–'80
% of Total U.S. Population	15.8	16.0	16.3	16.6	16.8	17.1	17.4	17.7	18.0	18.3
Allopathic Medicine	7.1	8.6	8.7	9.1	10.0	9.1	9.0	9.0	8.7	9.1
Osteopathy	—	2.4	2.8	1.8	3.4	3.9	4.0	4.0	4.4	4.5
Dentistry	—	6.1	6.2	6.6	6.6	6.9	6.9	7.1	6.7	7.5
Optometry[a]	—	2.1	2.5	3.1	3.4	3.7	3.5	3.3	3.1	3.0
Pharmacy	—	—	—	4.9	5.2	7.0	6.3	6.4	6.4	7.2
Podiatric Medicine	—	3.3	—	2.5	—	—	5.5	—	—	7.1
Veterinary Medicine[b]	—	2.6	2.6	3.0	2.9	3.3	3.8	3.8	4.1	4.0
Nursing[c]										
R.N. Program	—	10.8	—	—	12.6	—	—	11.2	—	—
L.P.N. Program	—	19.4	—	—	17.9	—	—	15.6	—	—

Continued

[a]Based upon total enrollment data for underrepresented minorities.
[b]Based upon total enrollment data for all minorities prior to academic year 1982–1983.
[c]Based upon first year enrollment data for all minorities.

SOURCE: Minorities and Women in the Health Fields, 1990 Edition; DHHS/PHS/HRSA personal communication, October 6, 1993.

Table 2-1. *Continued*

	'80–'81	'81–'82	'82–'83	'83–'84	'84–'85	'85–'86	'86–'87	'87–'88	'88–'89	'91–'92
% of Total U.S. Population	18.6	18.9	19.2	19.5	19.9	20.2	20.5	20.9	21.2	22.2
Allopathic Medicine	9.0	9.7	9.4	9.7	9.8	10.6	10.0	11.1	11.8	11.0
Osteopathy	4.4	4.5	4.8	5.7	6.5	5.2	6.5	6.2	—	7.1
Dentistry	7.6	8.7	8.9	9.0	10.4	11.4	13.6	15.2	15.1	12.5
Optometry[a]	3.3	3.6	4.4	5.0	5.2	5.8	—	6.2	—	9.4
Pharmacy	8.0	8.3	9.1	9.3	9.4	9.6	—	9.9	—	12.2
Podiatric Medicine	8.1	9.1	9.7	11.0	12.9	14.7	13.4	15.8	17.1	17.8
Veterinary Medicine[b]	4.6	4.8	4.7	4.7	4.5	5.4	5.6	5.4	6.3	5.8
Nursing[c]										
R.N. Program	13.5	—	—	12.9	12.7	14.6	—	—	—	13.5
L.P.N. Program	17.5	—	—	17.7	22.2	—	—	—	—	—

[a]Based upon total enrollment data for underrepresented minorities.
[b]Based upon total enrollment data for all minorities prior to academic year 1982–1983.
[c]Based upon first year enrollment data for all minorities.

SOURCE: Minorities and Women in the Health Fields, 1990 Edition; DHHS/PHS/HRSA personal communication, October 6, 1993.

Table 2-2. Minority Total Enrollments in Selected Health Professions Schools: Academic Year 1991–1992

Selected Health Professions School	TOTAL	Underrepresented Minorities	African American	Hispanic	Native American	Asian
		Number of Students				
Allopathic Medicine[a]	66,142	6,787	4,638	1,665	333	9,994
Osteopathic Medicine	7,012	549	236	276	37	685
Dentistry[a]	15,980	2,143	943	1,152	48	2,650
Pharmacy	23,482	2,485	1,531	867	87	2,755
Podiatric Medicine	2,247	402	233	161	8	201
Optometry	4,864	458	141	295	22	652
Nursing (RN)	237,598	30,578	21,529	7,349	1,700	6,947
Veterinary Medicine	8,440	495	192	257	46	141
Allied Health[b]	92,520	16,349	10,251	5,590	508	3,453
		Percent Distribution				
Allopathic Medicine[a]	100.0	10.3	7.0	5.8	0.5	15.1
Osteopathic Medicine	100.0	7.8	3.4	3.9	0.5	9.8
Dentistry[a]	100.0	13.4	5.9	7.2	0.3	16.6
Pharmacy	100.0	10.6	6.5	3.7	0.4	11.7
Podiatric Medicine	100.0	17.9	10.4	7.2	0.4	8.9
Optometry	100.0	9.4	2.9	6.1	0.5	13.4
Nursing (RN)	100.0	12.9	9.1	3.1	0.7	2.9
Veterinary Medicine	100.0	5.9	2.3	3.0	0.5	1.7
Allied Health[b]	100.0	17.7	11.1	6.0	0.5	3.7

[a] Data are for 1992–1993.
[b] Data are for 1990–1991 as reported by 2,882 CAHEA Accredited Programs. These data include 26 allied health occupations.

SOURCE: Bureau of the Health Professions, DHHS, 1993; AAMC, 1993.

The Bureau of Health Professions data gives some further analysis on the type of progress being made from the early 1970s through the mid/late 1980s, the last years for which comprehensive analysis was made available (HRSA, 1990). For example:

- While overall first-year enrollment in schools of osteopathic medicine almost tripled between 1971–1972 and 1987–1988, minority first-year enrollment increased tenfold during that time, from 2.4 percent to 6.2 percent of total first-year enrollment. Although all underrepresented groups remain well below parity, Hispanics have the largest proportional presence. However, the racial and ethnic enrollments in individual schools vary widely.
- In dentistry, as in medicine, the representation of minority women has been increasing at a faster rate than minority men. On a population parity basis, Hispanics and Native Americans are better represented than African Americans.

Even in dental schools where enrollment rates have increased among all minority groups, whites still have the highest enrollment rate and African Americans the lowest. African Americans have attrition rates 2.5 times higher than whites and Hispanics (American Dental Association, 1992). Nearly, three-quarters of African-American first-year students who withdraw say they do so for academic reasons; 57 percent of Hispanics and 47 percent of whites who withdraw also cite academic reasons (American Dental Association, 1992).

Dentistry consistently has one of the highest proportions of underrepresented minorities among all health professions. Given this fact, further study of ways to enhance dental programs may prove helpful not only to dentistry, but to the other health professions' efforts. The Institute of Medicine is currently undertaking an intensive study on dental education and oral health. Upon its release in 1994, the study will give recommendations as to how dental education might better respond to current problems and future challenges, including issues of racial and ethnic representation.

- The presence of underrepresented minorities in veterinary schools increased significantly between the years 1978–1979 and 1988–1989. While the overall increase in student enrollment was 5.2 percent, the minority matriculation rate increased by 77 percent. Tuskegee, a historically black institution, graduated 38 percent of all minority veterinary graduates in 1985–1986; only two schools, excluding Tuskegee, had more than 6 percent minority graduates.
- In optometry, minority students are further from reaching parity than in medicine or dentistry. Native Americans are well represented in optometry, but their total numbers are small.
- All minorities have made significant enrollment gains in schools of pharmacy. Minority enrollment has continued to rise steadily. As a percentage of the total, minority students have increased from 5.1 percent to 13.3 percent.
- First-year enrollments in schools of podiatry increased by more than 100

percent between 1971–1972 and 1986–1987. The overall percentage of minority first-year enrollment increased from 3.3 percent in 1971–1972 to 17.9 percent in 1991–1992. African-American and Hispanic enrollment increased at mainly steady rates; Native American representation was more erratic and small. In 1988–1989, African-American representation was closest to parity. Hispanics are not as well represented in podiatry as in other health professions.

• Total enrollment in education programs for registered nurses declined by 15.6 percent between academic years 1971–1972 and 1987–1988. During this same period, minority enrollment decreased 7.6 percent, but the proportion of minorities enrolled increased to 15.8 percent from 10.4 percent according to schools reporting the racial and ethnic composition of their students. Total enrollment for practical nurse programs, after a drop in the mid-1970s, remained consistently around the 21 percent level during this time. All minority groups remain significantly underrepresented in registered nurse programs. Among health careers, practical nurse programs continue to have the highest minority representation (HRSA, 1990).

As enrollment in nursing schools has declined along with financial resources, there have been increased efforts to recruit and retain students once deemed academically "high risk" into baccalaureate programs (Epps et al., 1993). But statistics compiled by the National League of Nursing illustrate the importance of developing adequate prematriculation and retention programs. By 1984, according to the League, 13 percent of those accepted into college nursing programs in the South were African American, but African Americans made up only 8 percent of the graduates of those programs (Epps et al., 1993).

Published programs in nursing schools, primarily those implemented and evaluated in the 1970s, are few and statistical evaluations are almost nonexistent; data consist usually of a qualitative review of questionnaire responses. A number of these evaluations, while limited, show some improvement in student retention and graduation rates as a result of various support programs. The presence or absence of a real faculty commitment toward enhancing minority participation has been shown to be closely related with achieving more positive results (Epps et al., 1993).

Some nursing schools have now begun more innovative and concerted programs to increase minority participation and retention in the health professions. Early evaluations of this strategy in nursing have been favorable, but there are as yet few published studies of their impact (Epps et al., 1993). Recently, there has been more of an effort on the part of nursing programs to bring so-called high-risk students along. These endeavors should be more closely examined.

Allied Health

The ethnic mix of students enrolled in schools of allied health generally reflects the ethnic mix of the U.S. population. In 1991–1992, African Americans represented 11 percent of total enrollments; Hispanics, 6 percent; and Native Americans, 0.5 percent. Among allied health personnel, which make up between 1 million and 4 million people (depending on how the field is defined), there are both highly educated people and people who have been trained on the job (for example, occupational therapists and home health aides) (IOM [Institute of Medicine], 1989). It is important to note that minorities are underrepresented in allied health fields that require more education (IOM, 1989).

Like other health professions schools, allied health schools have received federal funds under the Health Careers Opportunity Program, and these schools have often succeeded in recruiting enough minorities to double their minority enrollment (Epps et al., 1993). Belatedly, the schools have discovered that many of the new students are ill-prepared because of inadequate high school and college training in biology, chemistry, and physics (Epps et al., 1993). One survey, in 1992, found that more than one-half of the Hispanic and one-third of the African-American students were high risk because they had C or D grade point averages in the college courses they took before beginning their allied health studies (Epps et al., 1993).

Few data are available on programs to increase minority enrollment because school administrators have only recently begun collecting data for programs that were begun in the 1980s. There have been, however, recent increases in the number of minority students at schools receiving HCOP funds to both recruit and retain minorities in the schools of allied health (Epps et al., 1993).

FACTORS ASSOCIATED WITH MINORITY UNDERREPRESENTATION

A number of factors have been associated with minority underrepresentation in the health professions, particularly medicine. They include racism, lack of sustained funding for programs, lack of institutional commitment, and the effects of a significant legal ruling. These factors are examined in this section.

Overt Racism or Lack of Concern?

In surveys, students have said they faced little overt racism, but others found racism in medical school and said it had an influence on their careers (Reitzes and Elkhanialy, 1976; Wolkon and Yamamoto, 1978; Fullilove et al.,

1988). Why would these feelings persist even in schools working hard to admit and retain minority students? Jennings, in an article in the *Trotter Institute Review*, argues that the academic environment is no less hostile today to African-American students than it was in 1926, when W.E.B. Dubois described the attitude of the "northern institution toward the negro student [as] one which varies from tolerance to active hostility" (Jennings, 1989). The nation's educational leaders pay "lip service" to the idea of opening institutions of higher education to more minorities and deplore racial violence and harassment. But they may tolerate racism and racial insensitivity at their own institutions (Jennings, 1989). Others concede that a less-than-hospitable climate for minorities on many college campuses has played a role in diverting minority students from careers in the health professions (Petersdorf, 1991; Richardson and Skinner, 1991). Petersdorf points to "poor academic preparation prior to college" as the primary reason minority students drop out of the medical school pipeline (Petersdorf, 1991).

A study at the University of Rochester offers clues to why some academics view overt racism as "much less common" (Petersdorf, 1991), while others call such a perspective an example of a phenomenon noted by Martin Luther King, Jr.—"America fantasizes racial harmony" (King, 1967; Jennings, 1989).

The University of Rochester study of a year-long tutorial examined the interactions between minority medical students, staff, and faculty (Fullilove et al., 1988). Tutoring began only after students had failed their first year, months after they had begun to have academic problems. By the time the target students joined in a group tutorial specifically created for minority students, they distrusted the school (Geertsma, 1977).

Students in the program who had been told that their academic work was not up to par believed they were the objects of racially motivated put-downs. As a result, they did not respond to helpful suggestions for improving their academic performance. In their account of the study, Fullilove et al. suggested that faculty members had indirectly implied that the students lacked the intellectual resources to learn. The authors warned that this message is passed on to minority students from nursery school to graduate school (Fullilove et al., 1988). At all levels, most programs for minority students are remedial. Instead of learning to define and overcome what is holding them back in their studies, students often learn they are inferior and cannot succeed (Fullilove et al., 1988).

Problems in Funding

Against the backdrop of rising tuition, an unhealthy economy, and the declining public interest in providing minorities with equal rights to an education, students have had to rely on loans rather than scholarships to fund their educations (Ready and Nickens, 1993). Several studies indicate that rising tuition and the decline in scholarship money have been decisive factors in the decreasing minority enrollment in higher education, including the health professions schools (Jennings, 1989; NRC, 1989; Petersdorf, 1991). According to data collected by the National Medical Fellowships, Inc., the annual cost of a medical education in academic years 1981–1982 and 1987–1988 rose 80.3 percent at public schools and 55.5 percent at private schools (Johnson, 1990). Despite the daunting costs, however, many minority students are willing to shoulder the debt necessary to obtain an education in the health professions. However, medical students in particular too often make uninformed decisions about the medical schools they choose to attend and the manner in which they will pay for medical education (Johnson, 1990).

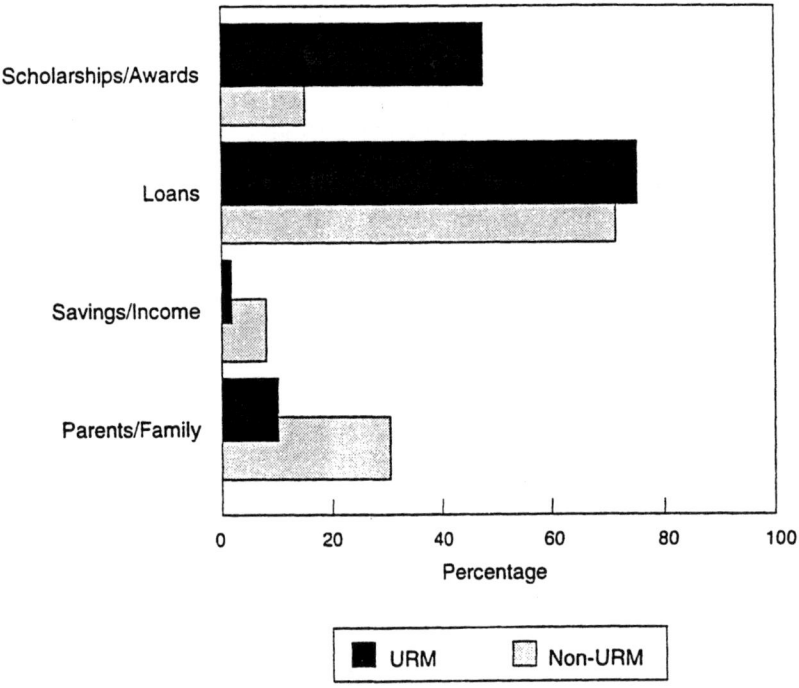

Figure 2-7. How matriculants will finance at least 25 percent of their medical school costs. SOURCE: Minority Students in Medical Education: Facts and Figures VII, AAMC, 1993.

As tuitions have risen, private philanthropy has cut back on its support for preparing minority students for careers in the health professions. During the 1970s and 1980s, the private foundations that funded efforts to enhance minority participation focused primarily on increasing the applicant pool (Epps et al.,

1993). Those programs had little impact, however, on the shortage of minorities in the health professions, and the foundations looked elsewhere for proved interventions, committed institutions, and careful selection of students (Robert Wood Johnson Foundation, 1987). Meanwhile, the federal government has shifted its financial aid resources into providing high-interest loans and programs that subsidize tuition costs in return for promises of public service after graduation, such as the National Health Service Corps (Epps et al., 1993; Ready and Nickens, 1993). It has been argued that in cutting back on its financial aid programs for students in higher education, the federal government has undermined racial diversity and access (Jennings, 1989).

In 1992, the average debt of minority students in medical school was $58,737, compared to $55,497 for other medical students (AAMC, 1993a). While this difference may not seem great, the size of the debt is much more likely to discourage a minority student whose family has little experience with earning enough to repay such large sums of money (Johnson, 1990; Cregler et al., 1993). Furthermore, current data show that 40 percent of underrepresented minority students have to rely on high-cost, unsubsidized loans, compared with 35 percent of all students (AAMC, 1993a).

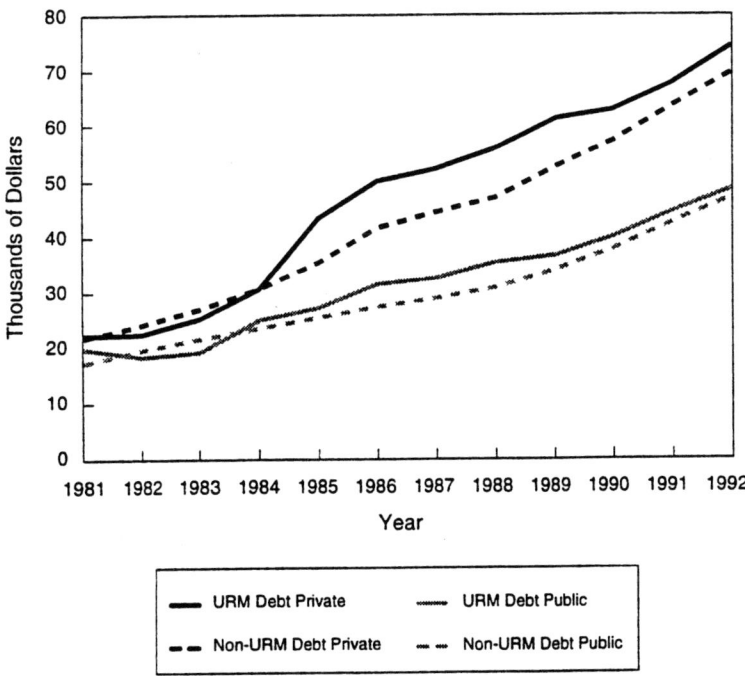

Figure 2-8. Average debt for indebted medical school graduates, 1981–1992. SOURCE: Minority Students in Medical Education: Facts and Figures VII, AAMC, 1993.

Lack of Institutional Commitment

There have been other reasons why well-intentioned efforts have failed to increase the number of underrepresented minorities in the sciences. Some key reasons most often cited by educators, government officials, researchers, and others are presented below (Sims, 1992).

- **Lack of real commitment from the top or from most faculty.**

Institutions often fail to integrate into their missions the goals of their minority programs. The programs are also often run by faculty members who have no real leadership role at their institutions and, thus, lack credibility and adequate resources to address the problems faced by minority students (Sims, 1992; Cregler et al., 1993; Ready and Nickens, 1993). There may indeed be a correlation between the way a medical school staffs its minority affairs office and how successful the school is at attracting minority students (Ready and Nickens, 1993). For example, medical schools that have no minority staff working on minority affairs issues tend to have low minority enrollment (Ready and Nickens, 1993). Furthermore, medical schools often show a lack of commitment to increasing minority enrollment by failing to include on admissions committees women and underrepresented minorities who might be sensitive to cultural differences (Edwards et al., 1990; Cregler et al., 1993).

Table 2-3. Staff Time Devoted to Minority Programs as Related to Underrepresented Minority Enrollment, 1991

FTE	Number of Schools	Average URM Matriculants (%)	Matriculant Representation Factor
<1	37	5.8	.36
1–1.9	25	8.7	.41
2–2.9	25	8.6	.58
≥3	25	11.3	.80

SOURCE: Ready, T.P., and Nickens, H.W. Inventory and Analysis of the Effectiveness of Strategies and Programs for Increasing Minority Participation in the Health Professions, 1993.

Despite improvements in the academic credentials of African-American applicants to medical school, African Americans have had substantially lower acceptance rates in recent years (Ready and Nickens, 1993). All three of the background papers prepared for the IOM committee called for further study of the falling matriculation rate for minorities, even when the recent upward trend in medical school enrollment for 1992 and 1993 is considered (Cregler et al.,

1993; Epps et al., 1993; Ready and Nickens, 1993). The major barrier for underrepresented minorities is getting accepted to medical school, and the greatest barrier to acceptance is the lack of academic preparation.

- **Colleges recruit unprepared minority students and then leave them to sink or swim.**

In the early 1970s, as the result of a second-rate education (particularly in math and sciences), underrepresented minorities on average had weaker academic credentials than other students accepted to college and health professions schools as they began their studies in what had been nearly all-white institutions (Johnson et al., 1975). This factor, combined with the psychological barriers noted below, contributed to the relatively high attrition rates among minority students (Ready and Nickens, 1993).

Health professions schools and other institutions all along the pipeline have struggled with helping students make up for gaps in their preparation, with varying degrees of success. Some schools, as discussed above, have tried remedial programs that may carry with them a stigma and a message that the student is destined to fail (Fullilove et al., 1988). Even today, students with little mathematics or science background are aggressively recruited to study science or engineering in college, then left to make their own way (Sims, 1992).

- **Programs ignore subtle psychological issues, such as low expectations on the part of teachers and counselors.**

High school and college teachers and guidance counselors often discourage their minority students from taking challenging courses in mathematics and science. There is a general assumption that minorities are not smart enough to handle the work (Sims, 1992).

Once minority students have succeeded in gaining admission to a health professions school, they must still handle cultural differences and biases and learn how to accommodate their cultures with the prevailing one at the majority institution. In many cases, when minority students experience difficulty during medical school, it is due to nonacademic reasons (Shea and Fullilove, 1985; Sedlacek, 1987).

Medical schools also have been slow to provide students with the mentors who can help guide career choices and help make the academic environment a more hospitable one. The failure of medical schools to increase the number of underrepresented minorities among their faculty has deprived minority students of role models and created another barrier to increasing the number of minority physicians (Cregler et al., 1993; Wilson and Kaczmarek, 1993). In 1992, minority faculty made up 3.5 percent of the 70,187 medical school faculty in the United States, compared to the 2.6 percent in 1982 (Jolley and Hudley, 1993). However, more than one-third of these faculty members either are teaching at minority medical schools or are on staff at minority medical centers (Wilson and Kaczmarek, 1993). Consequently, in 1992, underrepresented minorities comprised only 2.6 percent of full-time faculty at nonminority institutions (AAMC, 1993a).

- **Programs target college-age or older students instead of also going to the root of the problem in elementary and high schools.**

As far back as 1978, an AAMC task force recommended that medical schools establish "meaningful relationships with the colleges and senior high schools in their region to encourage, motivate and prepare students from racial minority groups for careers in medicine" (AAMC, 1978). Despite these recommendations, medical schools have made little effort to change their strategies for increasing minority enrollment (Ready and Nickens, forthcoming).

The schools had perhaps hoped that the pool of applicants would grow if minority college graduates could be encouraged to pursue careers in medicine. However, rapid growth in minority enrollment in bachelor's degree programs ended in the mid-1970s, and so did the expansion in the number of minorities in medical schools (Ready and Nickens, forthcoming).

- **Programs had vague or unrealistic goals.**

Even when they were implemented, programs to increase minority enrollment in the sciences at the undergraduate and graduate levels suffered from unrealistic expectations and lack of accountability (Sims, 1992). The programs expected too much from too many students in too short a period of time. Also, many of the programs failed to understand the complexity of the situation. Students from disadvantaged backgrounds had a lot of catching up to do, and the academic challenges they faced were complicated by the economic and environmental circumstances in which they found themselves. Had these programs been carefully evaluated, later initiatives could have anticipated and overcome previous failings more readily.

In the early days of federal funding under HCOP, evidence of success appeared because the numbers of minority students were increasing in the health professions schools funded under the program. But during the 1980s, program reports began to suggest that students were shown to have attained the objectives of the funded programs (Epps et al., 1993). More recently, attrition rates and the failure of programs to actually increase the number of minority health professionals have led private foundations into "making sure the program sponsor is truly committed to the recruitment and retention of minority students" (Robert Wood Johnson Foundation, 1987).

Regents of California v. *Bakke*

In the early 1970s, 16 percent of medical schools maintained separate admissions committees, and many also set aside a specified number of seats for minority applicants. In 1974, these practices at the University of California at

Davis were challenged in the state courts by an unsuccessful white applicant to that school. Four years later, the U.S. Supreme Court said such practices were unconstitutional. Race, the court said, could be considered as only one factor in admissions decisions. This decision, taken against the backdrop of declining societal interest and commitment to opening up opportunities for minorities, is thought to have contributed to the stagnation in minority enrollment in health professions schools (Cregler et al., 1993).

Individual and Community Responsibilities

Minority families, communities, and institutions must share the responsibility for changing the system, working with nonminority policymakers and educators (Action Council on Minority Education, 1990). All students have a major responsibility for their education and the level of effort put forth to learn even in the poorest of circumstances. Minority students, in particular, must set their sights high. In so doing they will need the support of family and community. Such support may not always be possible because of the family's own limited educational opportunities or other societal deprivations. Especially in such cases, support must be available from an extended family in the form of a teacher, or mentor, or the larger community (Epps et al., 1993).

CONCLUSION

The current stagnation in minority enrollment in the health professions exists despite a significant commitment to minority recruitment on the part of many institutions and individuals. In some cases, their efforts have been successful, showing that the problem is not insurmountable. There are still some schools, however, whose failure to increase the number of minority graduates shows a lack of commitment. It is to those institutions that Chapter 3 is addressed. In Petersdorf's words, "It is fair to say that the schools that have been successful in producing a relatively large number of underrepresented minority graduates have benefitted from strong commitment to minority recruitment by their leadership" (Petersdorf, 1991).

3

Lessons from Successful Programs

A number of foundations and state and federal agencies have tried to solve the problems outlined in Chapter 2. Nonetheless, the designers of new intervention programs may find that few models have been rigorously and effectively evaluated. Throughout the various levels of the educational system, however, there are examples of well-regarded efforts to increase the number of underrepresented minority students in medicine and other health professions. Some of these programs are described in this chapter.

The programs chosen by the committee illustrate efforts to confront the issue; they do not constitute a definitive list of answers. Programs at different academic levels, beginning with the medical school, are presented.

In light of what has been learned from these programs and others over the past 20 years, researchers now understand many of the factors that help in attracting minority students and in retaining them in courses that lead toward health careers and, later, in assisting them at the health professions schools. Enough is now known to design and implement programs with a high likelihood of success. The most important message each of these programs offers is that "if the gap between the potential and the actual participation of minorities in medicine is not bridged, it will be because as a nation we have held the blueprints, yet not constructed the plan" (Robert Wood Johnson Foundation, 1987). The same can be said for the other health professions.

MEDICAL SCHOOL LEVEL

The Admissions Process

Until recently, the University of Tennessee at Memphis ranked near the bottom one-fourth of U.S. medical schools in recruiting underrepresented minorities. The school now ranks among the top one-fourth of medical schools in terms of African-American student enrollment.

The school's success lay in a series of steps taken by the administration. It made an institutional commitment to adequate funding, added more minorities to the admissions committee, and sent its admissions personnel to a workshop conducted by the Association of American Medical Colleges (AAMC) to learn about noncognitive variables that influence successful completion (Taylor et al., 1990).

Known as the Simulated Minority Admissions Exercise, the AAMC program was developed to help admissions committees recognize minority students who would succeed in medical school despite relatively low test scores and grade point averages (GPAs). The workshop, whose techniques have been applied at medical schools throughout the United States, taught the admissions committee at the University of Tennessee to look for the following noncognitive variables in students who were being considered for admission: a positive self-concept, an ability to focus on long-range goals, a supportive person in the student's life, leadership qualities, a background of community service, and demonstrated medical interests.

Fostering Academic Careers

Harvard Medical School's Minority Faculty Development Program sponsors visiting clerkships for fourth-year and qualified third-year minority medical students. The students may take 1-month clerkships in any discipline at any of the 13 hospitals affiliated with the medical school.

The goal of the program is to make minority students aware of the opportunities open to them in academic medicine, to increase the likelihood they will choose academic training programs for their internships and residencies, and to increase the number of minority students applying to hospital training programs affiliated with Harvard Medical School.

Each participant is assigned a faculty advisor and is enrolled in the medical school's Exchange Clerkship Program.

Cosponsored by Bristol-Myers Squibb Company and the Commonwealth Fund, the Fellowships Program in Academic Medicine for Minority Students has allowed more than 200 minority medical students to spend up to 3 months working on research projects under the guidance of experienced biomedical researchers. The program's goal is to encourage more minority students to consider careers in academic medicine. An application must include a statement about the student's career goals and a letter of commitment from the proposed mentor outlining the research program and the role the mentor will play in guiding the student during his or her medical training.

Every year, 35 fellowships are awarded to qualified second- and third-year medical students who are U.S. citizens of African-American, mainland Puerto Rican, Mexican American, or Native American descent. Participants each receive an award of $6,000, from which the mentor may draw up to $2,000 to cover the costs of the internship. The program provides each fellow with a close-up view of academic medicine and access to a major biomedical library.

Initial results of an AAMC survey of this program showed several positive outcomes. Fellowship recipients were more likely to take part in research activities in medical school than any other minority or nonminority student interested in a career in academic medicine. Fellows were also more likely to have authored, or coauthored, research papers in medical school than were other classmates who shared their career interests.

As they continued their chosen careers, almost 90 percent of the students who participated in the program said they called on their mentors for guidance and support. The development of the relationship between these medical students and the noted academic physicians and researchers who mentor them is considered the key element of success in the fellowship program (AAMC, 1993b).

The program is administered by National Medical Fellowships, Inc., which provides need-based scholarships and special programs for underrepresented minorities.

Faculty Development

The Robert Wood Johnson Foundation Minority Medical Faculty Development Program offers minority physicians 4-year, postdoctoral research fellowships. Each of the fellows must have demonstrated superior academic and clinical skills and be committed to a career in academic medicine.

The foundation provides each fellow with an annual stipend of up to $50,000 and a $25,000 grant to support research. Working under the supervision of a senior faculty member at an academic health center, the fellow spends at least 70 percent of his or her time in a research activity.

POSTBACCALAUREATE PROGRAMS

Among the most promising experiments to increase the pool of qualified minority applicants are those that attempt to bridge the gap between college and medical school. The programs vary in length from a summer experience to a full postgraduate year.

Three years ago the federal Health Career Opportunities Program (HCOP) began funding postbaccalaureate programs in 14 medical schools. Minority and disadvantaged students who have unsuccessfully applied to medical school are enrolled in a 1-year course of study. They receive training in basic sciences and learn study skills. If academic performance is satisfactory, they are admitted automatically to the next year's entering class. About 100 minority and disadvantaged students are admitted to medical schools every year in this way.

Michigan State University (MSU) offers the Advanced Baccalaureate Learning Experience (ABLE) program for a small group of students from underrepresented and disadvantaged backgrounds (Cregler et al., 1993). Over a summer and the academic year that follows, students receive the necessary preparation they need to gain entry into the College of Human Medicine at MSU. If the students complete the program successfully, they are admitted automatically into the college of medicine. The 7 to 10 students chosen to take part in the program must also attend a 6-week summer session just before they matriculate into the college.

COLLEGE PROGRAMS

Many of the programs to increase minority representation at the college level are based on the Professional Development Program (PDP) of the University of California at Berkeley. The program, which was developed in 1978, has helped hundreds of minority students do well in calculus. Its founders examined the study habits of Asian students, who "coalesced into loosely knit social/study groups. . . . Their success appeared to be a direct result of their participation in group learning activities" (Fullilove et al., 1988). Their findings led to the creation of the Professional Development Program Mathematics Workshop.

The PDP sells itself to students as an honors program, because the participants agree to strive for honors in all subjects. Students are organized in small groups and work together on difficult problems assigned at the start of each workshop. As the students explain their findings to each other, they become more articulate and more comfortable with the material. A camaraderie develops along with the skills that have allowed participants to outperform fellow Asian and white students in freshman mathematics at the university. The participants also earn higher mean grades in the university's rigorous first-year calculus course for engineering and science majors. Two-thirds of the students in the program graduate. This success is attributed to two factors. The students learn to study "efficiently and effectively with others . . . and workshop membership provides students with stable, long-lasting friendships that serve as anchors in the University community" (Fullilove et al., 1988).

The Science Educational Enhancement Services Program in Pomona, California, uses faculty advisors, tutors, group study centers, student clubs, and academic excellence workshops to help minorities flourish in the science fields.

The program, sponsored by the California State Polytechnic University, tries to foster a sense of community and to help students with their academic work. Students attend academic excellence workshops in subjects such as math, chemistry, physics, and engineering, which are based on the PDP. The sense of community plays an important role in overcoming the sense of social isolation felt by many minority students.

The Meyerhoff Scholars, a 4-year-old program at the University of Maryland, Baltimore County, takes the best African-American students from high schools in Maryland and turns them into scientists and engineers. The program, which provides scholarships and free room and board to promising students, has produced more African-American students with A's and B's in science and engineering than has been done by the university in its history. The students have a GPA of 3.5, and were chosen for their academic abilities. Most of them scored in the top 2 percent in the math section of the Scholastic Aptitude Test (SAT). From the beginning, the Meyerhoff scholars have shared a dormitory and have been encouraged to study as a group. The goal is to overcome the isolation felt by some African-American students who are studying at predominantly white institutions.

The Meyerhoff Scholars program began with a gift from Baltimore philanthropists Robert and Jane Meyerhoff. It now has a budget of $4 million, which is partly funded by the National Aeronautics and Space Administration and the National Science Foundation (NSF). The program's first six graduates have been accepted on full scholarships for graduate study at schools such as Princeton University, the University of Pennsylvania, and Northwestern University (Leff, 1993).

Half of the students at Xavier University in New Orleans are studying natural sciences. With 3,100 students, the relatively small institution is second in the nation at putting African Americans into medical school. Among its efforts, the university conducts a sequence of summer programs for high school students in grades 9 to 12.

Almost 50 percent of Xavier's students graduate with degrees in mathematics and science, compared to a national average of 7 percent. School administrators argue that the strong science background they provide to premedical students is necessary to free them to confront the psychological, nonacademic pressures many minorities face in their first year of medical school.

Xavier provides "a clear, unambiguous vision of the primary objective of the program—the preparation of students to enter post-graduate studies leading to a career in the health professions" (Ready and Nickens, forthcoming). The school places great importance on introductory science courses, a point at which many colleges lose students who had been interested in science. Students are encouraged to study in groups and seek help from professors. The premedical office monitors each student's progress and works hard to prevent the student from dropping out of the program. Xavier maintains an unusual amount of cross-disciplinary collaboration and centralized control over curriculum. A group of faculty from several science departments meets regularly to discuss ways of improving the quality of instruction.

The summer enrichment programs in mathematics, chemistry, and biology are known collectively as the Summer Science Academy. A fourth program called Stress on Analytic Reasoning (SOAR) is a 4-week summer program that acts as a bridge to college courses. Students work on building their vocabulary and on increasing their problem-solving skills. Through laboratory work they learn methods of discovery, experimentation, and concept building.

College-Level Summer Program

The Minority Medical Education Program (MMEP) of the Robert Wood Johnson Foundation was designed to help promising, highly motivated minority (college) students gain admission to medical schools. Begun 5 years ago, the summer program at seven medical schools around the country provides experience in both the academic and the practical aspects of medicine and assigns each student to work with a mentor. Most students are introduced to both the clinical and the research sides of medicine. The program was developed after analysis of the foundation's 17 years of experience in funding projects for minority health professions students. The objective was to include in the MMEP the components that have been most effective in preparing students for medical school admission.

The MMEP helps students prepare for the Medical College Admissions Test and sharpen their skills in biology, mathematics, and problem solving. Students also learn to understand the medical school application process and how to finance a medical school education.

Since its inception, the program has received more than 6,000 applications and has enrolled more than 2,900 students. Applicants must have completed at least 1 year of college and have a GPA of 2.75 overall and 3.00 in the sciences. Many of the participants subsequently gained admission to medical school.

Faculty Development

To institutionalize programs for students, it is sometimes necessary to focus on faculty development. An example of one such effort is the Minority ACCESS to Research Careers Program. It is one of several programs supported by the National Institutes of Health (NIH) to encourage biomedical research training for students and faculty members at 4-year colleges and universities with large minority populations. The Faculty Fellowship component provides opportunities for advanced research training to full-time faculty members. The program also provides 12-month stipends to outstanding teacher-scientists to visit minority institutions, and includes an Honors Undergraduate Research Training component, which helps to interest undergraduates in biomedical research.

UNIVERSITY OUTREACH

Some colleges and universities have begun programs to reach out to communities around them. The Minority High School Summer Research Apprentice Program (MHSSRAP) is funded by the NIH and is designed to foster interest in science and mathematics among minority youth. Students accepted into the program earn money while performing laboratory work with biomedical researchers who act as their mentors.

The program was expanded several years ago to include high school teachers as part of the teaching team. More than 3,000 students and 600 teachers have participated in the program.

At the Medical College of Georgia, every one of the students in its NIH-funded MHSSRAP program has gone on to college. Almost 65 percent of those students who earned undergraduate degrees pursued careers in medicine or research.

The same program at the University of Alabama at Birmingham has grown from 18 students in 1989 to 60 students in the 1993 summer session. Most of the students are African American, as are the five high school teachers who supplement the work of the mentors. The 12-year-old program is so well known that the university does little to publicize it. Last year, for example, 250 students applied for the 60 slots in the program. The program chooses two-thirds of its participants because they have excelled academically. One-third of the participants are picked after interviews show them to have other qualities that compensate for their academic weaknesses.

As an offshoot of this program, the university has started a 4-week, graduate-level summer session for high school teachers to improve their skills in teaching biology.

In 1991, the University of California at San Francisco, in collaboration with the San Francisco Unified School District, developed a 4-year program to introduce a hands-on science curriculum to elementary school teachers in the local public schools entitled "City Science." The purpose of the program is to increase the involvement of the scientific community in the life of the elementary school child.

Funded by the National Science Foundation, and with supplemental grants from the Genentech Foundation for Biomedical Sciences, the program each year trains 100 elementary school teachers of kindergarten through fifth grade. During the summer the teachers take a 20-day course in teaching the curricula, followed by monthly, all-day sessions on Saturday during the school year. The sessions address techniques and problems associated with hands-on science instruction; how to do science in cooperative groups; how to couple hands-on science with hands-on assessment; and how to integrate science with writing, reading, and mathematics.

The course is taught by "master teachers," each of whom is assigned a scientist for help in improving and expanding the lesson. The teachers who take the course are required to teach the material they learned during the summer to their classes; a full-time science resource teacher evaluates the teachers' performances. During the school year, the scientists assigned to the program help the teachers in the classroom and serve as role models to the students.

The program designers hope to create a "large team of lead teachers" who will help other local public school teachers improve the quality of the science taught in the schools.

The University of California at Berkeley, in partnership with Oakland Technical High School, developed the MESA program, for Mathematics, Engineering, Science Achievement, to increase the number of minority students in science-related fields. Almost all of the first 25 students in the program, who were mostly poor and African American, went on to graduate from 4-year colleges. The founders of the program used the Socratic method, asking questions to make sure the students understood basic concepts and requiring the students to work together in study groups.

Today MESA reaches 14,000 California students in grades three through college. Participants are required to take challenging courses and to submit to intensive tutoring. They are also encouraged to develop a peer group that says "it's okay to be a good student." In addition to their work during the school year, students in the program spend every Saturday for 2 months in the summer studying English, science, and mathematics (Gibbons, 1992b).

The program has produced notable results. More than 70 percent of the high school students who participate go on to 4-year colleges, compared to a 13 percent college enrollment rate for minorities statewide. At the college level, the MESA Minority Engineering Program (MEP) is responsible for two-thirds of the bachelor's degrees awarded to African Americans, Hispanics, and Native Americans in California, producing a total of 600 engineers in 1992.

Most of the college and high school students in the MESA program are either African American or Mexican American; a small percentage is Puerto Rican and Native American. More than half the students in the program are female.

The program is supported by the state, school districts, and private foundations, with contributions of offices and staff from the universities that sponsor MESA in the local schools. The California business community has also played an important role. In 1990, for example, corporations contributed nearly $2 million in in-kind and monetary support to MESA programs (Carnegie Corporation, 1990).

HIGH SCHOOL PROGRAM

In 1981, Ventures in Education, with funding from the Josiah Macy, Jr., Foundation, began in five high schools around the country to give average minority and economically disadvantaged students the academic background necessary for acceptances to major colleges and universities. The program, which has now expanded to 83 schools in seven states and the District of Columbia, insists that each participating student take 4 years of science and mathematics, in an effort to encourage students to follow careers in science and the health professions.

To satisfy counseling and tutoring needs, each participating school agrees to extend the school day by at least one period; to keep program students together as a group throughout their high school years in order to reinforce a "culture of achievement"; to prepare the students properly for SAT and other standardized tests; and to offer advanced placement courses in biology, calculus, English, and social studies. The schools also agree to provide highly personalized and intensive guidance to program participants in their academic and personal lives.

Of the 1,036 participating students who graduated from high school in 1991, 95 percent enrolled in 4-year colleges, and of those who have been in college for 1 year or more, 45 percent are majoring in the sciences. Close to 41 percent have earned a GPA of 3.00 or better.

The Ventures program describes its role as that of a coach to the schools—encouraging, cheering, and cajoling so that all administrators and teachers perform at their best. In addition to support from the Macy Foundation, the program receives funding from several other sources, including the NSF and the U.S. Department of Education.

COMPREHENSIVE PROGRAMS

Unlike most of the programs in place around the country, the Chicago Area Health and Medical Careers Program (CAHMCP) is a comprehensive effort that starts in sixth grade and moves up through doctoral programs in the health care professions. The CAHMCP, which currently has about 1,000 participants, is a cooperative project offered by seven area medical schools to increase the number of qualified minority applicants. The program receives funding from a combination of sources: federal and state governments, private foundations, and the medical schools involved in the program.

The program identifies and recruits its participants early in their school years and provides structured academic, financial, and social support until the students have obtained a doctorate in one of the health care professions. In 1987, realizing that it was getting more difficult to identify and recruit young students into its high school program, CAHMCP began its Young Scientist Program to target minority students from grades six through nine who display exceptional interest and ability in the sciences. The program first recruited 23 Chicago elementary and junior high schools whose staffs, in turn, nominated students to the Young Scientist Program. For 4 to 5 weeks every summer, 350 sixth through ninth graders in the program take part in hands-on group projects in the chemistry, physics, and biology laboratories of local colleges. The program goes on to provide instruction and support to these students throughout their academic careers. CAHMCP is one of the sites of the Minority Medical Education Program of the Robert Wood Johnson Foundation.

In 12 years of effort, CAHMCP claims that 98 percent of the participants who enter the program at the high school level or earlier earn their baccalaureate degree within 5 years after entering college. According to program literature, 48 percent of the students who took part in the program from 1980 to 1985 went either to medical school or to another health professions school. Another 12 percent have graduated from or are now attending law school (Chicago Area Health and Medical Careers Program, 1992).

The Charles R. Drew University of Medicine and Science in Los Angeles oversees a comprehensive program that begins with 3-year-old children at a university-administered Head Start program and continues to work with area students through high school, college, medicine, and postgraduate training in the health professions.

Known as the Extended Science Pipeline, the program uses state, federal, and private funds to give students a practical understanding of science, as well as counseling, tutoring, mentoring, job training, career placement, financial assistance, and scholarships. In elementary school and junior high school, students take part in the Saturday Science Academy, which exposes them to science in both the laboratory and the classroom. Parents attend a series of workshops and seminars to reinforce the decision they made in enrolling their children in the program.

The King/Drew Medical Magnet High School is located on the campus of the university. The university says that 90 percent of the graduates of the magnet school go on to college and compete well in national, state, and local scholastic competition (Charles R. Drew University of Medicine and Science, 1992).

The Center for Educational Achievement at the university also provides for a series of summer workshops for high school students to guide them into the study of medicine and related health professions. The Allied Health Careers Opportunity Program (AHCOP), for example, sponsors a 6-week summer science institute and provides tutoring and counseling to students interested in studying, or already studying, in a school of allied health.

Under the umbrella of its Minority and School Based Programs, Baylor College of Medicine in Houston, Texas, administers, or is a major partner, in 18 different initiatives at the elementary, secondary, and undergraduate college levels. Baylor has put its greatest effort into the high school level. It founded the High School for the Health Professions in 1972 in the basement of the medical school. The high school now has its own building and has an enrollment of 750 students.

Between 1975 and 1990, 2,581 people had graduated from the school. According to a 1990 survey of the 1986 graduates, 4 percent had gone on to medical school or were physicians at the time of the survey, six times the nation's average for minority high school students (Butler et al., 1991). Nationally, high school graduates entering medical school make up only 0.6 percent of all graduates. Ninety-two percent of the 1986 graduates had gone on to college, and 75 percent of those attending had majored in science or in a health discipline. Baylor also participates in the Robert Wood Johnson Minority Medical Education Program to prepare undergraduates for medical school.

With funding from the NSF and various other sources, Baylor is also developing, testing, and overseeing the implementation of a new science curriculum for grades seven and eight. In partnership with Rice University, Baylor also sponsors a program that brings 30 grade school teachers to Baylor to learn to do hands-on science projects in their classrooms. Upon returning to their respective schools, the teachers then teach what they have learned to their colleagues.

SUMMARY

The efforts described above share many elements that can contribute to a successful program to increase the number of minority youth channeled into the health professions. At a 1992 forum hosted by the Kaiser Family Foundation on preparing minorities for the health professions, participants listed the ingredients without which a program could not succeed (Ready and Nickens, forthcoming):

- solid academic preparation at the precollege level;
- a high-caliber undergraduate college curriculum taught in a supportive environment;
- experiential, hands-on learning opportunities;
- availability of accurate, reliable counseling and resource materials;
- financial security; and
- social access (to overcome the pressures of "culture shock" and isolation often felt by minorities studying in majority institutions).

Students who lack social access to the institution, for example, may find themselves isolated and unable to continue their studies, regardless of how talented they might be and how well their financial needs have been met.

The programs discussed above create among their student participants a culture of success, in which the students move forward as a group. The focus is not on one or two stars, but on the successful completion of the program by each student.

Comprehensive "pipeline" programs represent an important alternative for the future. No one institution can alone change the social and educational system that has led to the underrepresentation of minorities in science, particularly in the health professions. Academic medical centers, under the leadership of the AAMC, are being encouraged to focus on themselves as "an integral part of the communities they serve" (Petersdorf, 1991). The AAMC "Project 3000 by 2000" envisions increasing the number of minority students in medical school through both short-term and long-term strategies. Medical schools, for example, would work with 4-year colleges to decompress the preclinical years, allowing students to take courses at both the undergraduate campus and the medical school during the senior year of college. Among the long-term projects suggested by the AAMC for its members is the creation of magnet health science high schools that would operate in partnership with colleges and medical schools to "create an integrated educational pathway" (Petersdorf, 1991). Such partnerships would give students the chance to take part in a rigorous curriculum in a hospitable environment, while providing the students with mentors and role models who would give relevance to the students' academic work.

4

Sharing Visions and Working Toward the Future

A vision that inspires people and ennobles a cause can transform dreams into reality. But one needs builders to realize a vision, builders who can develop ideas and movements, who can mobilize the talents and resources required to succeed. When the vision is clear and the impulse to succeed is strong, builders can create structures that endure.

As noted in several sections of this report, many laudable and durable building blocks to help raise the presence of minorities in the health professions are now in place, established over the last decades by government, the academic sector, and a number of foundations. But these worthwhile efforts, often working independently, over a limited period of time, or focused primarily at the later stages of the educational and training pathway, have been insufficient. We have yet to build the infrastructure and momentum to produce and sustain an adequate number of minority professionals among the ranks of America's clinicians, researchers, and teachers. Minorities in the health professions remain significantly underrepresented.

The Institute of Medicine's Committee on Increasing Minority Participation in the Health Professions envisions a health professions workforce for the future that looks more like America. The nation needs a new set of policies, programs, and priorities that can lead to a new approach to training minorities for the health professions, one that both celebrates and reflects America's changing demographic and economic profile.

There is today a bright window of opportunity to revitalize and move forward this nation's stalled commitment to enhancing minority participation in medicine and other health careers. Such optimism derives from several factors. There is new emphasis on investing in the domestic agenda, with a special focus on improving the education and skills of America's future workforce. Reform of the nation's health care system has become a political and economic priority.

The administration's vision for health care reform calls for the "creation of a new health workforce," and enhanced investment in "recruiting and supporting the education of health professionals from population groups underrepresented in the field" (American Health Security Act, 1993).

The current call for systemic change is compelling academic health centers and other institutions involved in education for the health professions to reassess future health workforce needs within a context of universal access and the health care needs of a more diverse society. The problem of dwindling access and declining coverage has brought into sharper relief the special health needs of underserved Americans, of whom a disproportionate number are minorities. Further, there is every indication that any reform strategy will provide incentives for enlarging the ranks of primary caregivers, nurses, and allied health professionals who enter community practice, a focus that represents promising career opportunities for minorities.

To meet the needs for health care, education, and research in an increasingly diverse society, the committee tried to formulate a strategy that would ensure a significant increase and a continuous supply of minority health professionals. The committee believed it critical to recommend greater emphasis on the "throughput"* of the educational process and on programs that will significantly increase the number of minorities prepared academically to pursue careers in medicine and science. Past reliance on stand-alone, rather than integrated, programs has nourished only a few institutions that compete for a small number of talented minority students and faculty. A greater presence of minorities in the health professions in clinical practice and research cannot, however, be reached by the field of medicine alone. Energized, sustained, and concerted strategies must involve the other health professions as well, including dentistry, optometry, pharmacy, podiatric medicine, veterinary medicine, nursing, and the growing field of allied health.

The committee calls **for a more systematic, strategic, and sustained effort to ensure the continuous flow of minority students qualified to choose careers in the health professions.** Any substantial improvement in minority enrollment in health profession's schools can occur only if the pipeline expands and more minority students gain the opportunity for solid academic preparation in a supportive environment, beginning well before high school. The fundamental cause of underrepresentation of minorities in health professions schools is an inadequate number of academically qualified and near-qualified students interested in health

---

*The concept of "throughput" is derived from *The Goal: A Process of Ongoing Improvement*, written by Eliyahu Goldratt and Jeff Cox (1986). This widely revered treatise/novel on modern industry and new global principles of manufacturing describes a process for ongoing growth and improvement in industry, education, and science.

(Baratz et al., 1985). Many past programs and strategies have relied too heavily on supplementary enrichment and recruitment programs for advanced premedical and postgraduate students. They have failed to address the root cause—the need to develop the applicant pool at earlier stages of the educational process.

While searching for intervention programs that emphasize a systematic, integrated approach, the committee identified a model developed by the American Association for the Advancement of Science (AAAS) as part of its recent report *Women, Minorities, and Persons with Physical Disabilities in Science and Engineering* (Matyas and Malcom, 1991). This model incorporates many of the features the committee believes essential for effective action in this arena (see Figure 4-1). Its underlying strategy is to move toward **changing the structure and the environment of the system, in contrast to isolated interventions aimed primarily at helping students or faculty from underrepresented groups fit into, adjust to, or negotiate the existing system.**

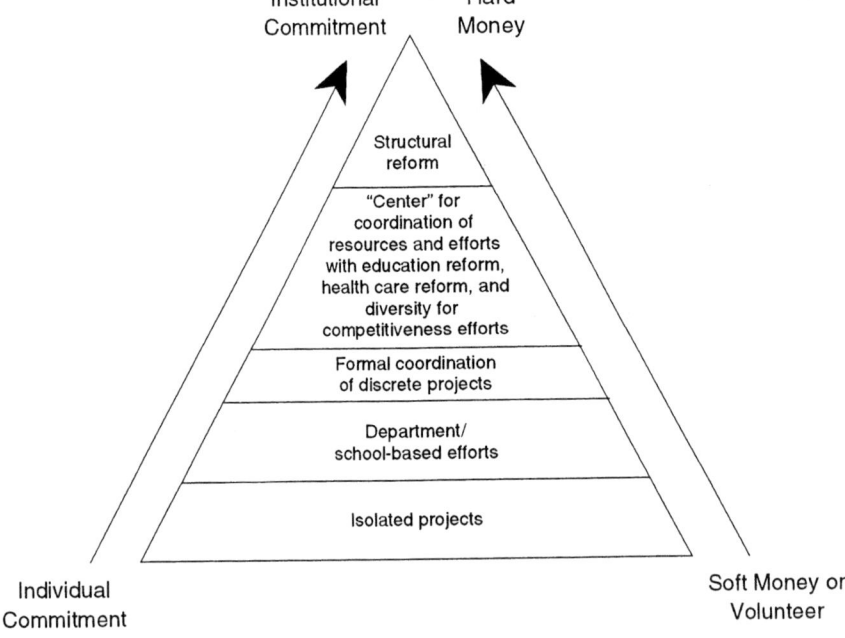

Figure 4-1. Model for the evolution of intervention programs. SOURCE: Modified from Matyas, M.L., and Malcom, S.M. Women, Minorities, and Persons with Physical Disabilities in Science and Engineering. American Association for the Advancement of Science, 1991. Reprinted with permission.

The model's proponents contend that "only by moving from ancillary activities aimed at helping students survive the current educational climate to changing the climate in which the students are educated, can we significantly affect the participation of minorities in health and science careers" (Matyas and Malcom, 1991). **Collaboration and broadened, sustained commitment from all of society's institutions and organizations that relate to the educational process must characterize future efforts to increase minority participation in professional careers.**

In applying the AAAS model to the goal of broadening the landscape of minority participation, **current isolated projects would become linked into a national educational network committed to ensuring an increasing and continuous supply of minority health professionals.** Instead of seeking merely to remedy educational deficits at the level of the professional school, the university would establish linkages with colleges in an effort to increase the supply of well-qualified candidates for the applicant pool. The colleges would, in turn, form partnerships with several high schools, and the high schools would team up with elementary schools. At the lower levels, the system would be broad based and focused on improved science and math learning, with the understanding that students would be "lost" to other professions. Evidence suggests, however, that even under these circumstances the throughput of minority candidates in the health professions is significantly increased.

The "center" for coordination of resources could be formed within the private sector by a consortium of health professions associations, such as the American Medical Association (AMA) and the American Dental Association (ADA), and managed in a way that would facilitate access to the many pathways that lead to health careers. Such a center could be the clearinghouse for information about resources that currently exist, but are scattered and little known. It would also help to disseminate information on national educational standards, advances in educational reform, and issues related to health care.

BUILDING THE VISION

All programs and interventions that contribute to a plan for enlarging the pool of minority health professionals must embody a number of important principles. They include improved mathematics and science learning, commitment to excellence, collaborative efforts, value on diversity, a constructive attitude for learning, culturally sensitive communications, mentoring, improved evaluation and dissemination, better resources, and attention to minority health.

Improved Mathematics and Science Learning

The committee encourages education reform that stresses a strong science and math foundation.

Over the past 10 years, efforts to strengthen the foundation for math and science learning have had disappointing results (Ratchford, 1992). Data show that students of all races filter out of science and math, so that only a fraction of interested high school students—1.4 percent—earn a Ph.D. degree. The minority pipeline, smaller to begin with, narrows even more sharply than that of the total population. As noted in Chapter 2, only 0.4 percent of minority students emerge with a Ph.D. degree in science or engineering. Studies comparing science and math students in industrialized countries consistently find U.S. students near the bottom, or dead last, bad news in a technology-driven world (Competitiveness Policy Council, 1993).

To reverse this trend, effective strategies must focus on making science and mathematics more accessible to all students, and especially to minorities and women. Establishing these competencies early in the educational process will help develop a cadre of minorities qualified to exercise choices about professional health career paths, including those of clinical practice, teaching, and research.

To understand America's poor standing in math and science, educators are increasingly pointing to the way these disciplines are taught, rather than to the inadequate ability of students. Teachers who are well trained and enthusiastic about their subject, who are effective communicators, who can advise, mentor, and encourage, are especially important in motivating minority students to pursue graduate study in science. The committee also sees the need to create a more inclusive academic environment for math and science training, one that incorporates understanding and appreciation of diversity as part of the effective teaching of these disciplines.

An academic environment that allows only the select to succeed is counter to the traditions of U.S. science and engineering. Asked by President Franklin D. Roosevelt to propose a plan to develop scientific talent, Massachusetts Institute of Technology engineer and presidential advisor, Vannever Bush, and his distinguished contemporaries responded, "We are not interested in the elect. We think it is much the best plan . . . that opportunity be extended to all kinds and conditions of men whereby they can better themselves. This is the American way; this is the way the United States has become what it is. We think it is very important that circumstances be such that there be no ceilings, other than ability itself to intellectual ambition. We think it is very important that every boy and girl know that, if he shows that he has what it takes, the sky is the limit" (Bush, 1945). **Faculty members teaching science must be convinced that recruiting minority students to math and science, not weeding them out, is in the national interest and should be an important priority.**

Commitment to Excellence

The committee urges a shift in perspective to an achievement model for minority education, with all educational institutions developing specific goals and implementation plans for inclusion and excellence.

Only when significant value is placed on excellence and achievement, can effective strategies and programs be realized. A growing call for excellence should join with goals of racial diversity and access. As the face of America's population rapidly changes, it is no longer appropriate to define quality and excellence in education separate from the need to prepare students for the complex economic, social, educational, and cultural issues they will face in the world of work, family, and community (Jennings, 1989). A broader orientation toward excellence pertains especially to the education and training of future health professionals who are asked to understand and relate to the special needs of patients from many different racial and ethnic backgrounds.

The importance of encouraging minorities to reach for lofty goals and giving them the confidence to achieve them cannot be overstated. Too many minority youth today are thwarted in their aspirations by perceptions that link minorities to high risk of scholastic failure. Remedial programs frequently drain the spirit of students, erode their self-confidence, and place too much emphasis on "getting through." They emphasize weaknesses. It is much better to focus on strengths.

Collaborative Efforts

For our minority youth, structures and incentives for collaborative work and study are essential building blocks for fostering improved learning of science and mathematics for underrepresented groups.

Capable students who switch out of science frequently cite science's "culture of competition" as an important factor in their decisions (Kahn, 1992). Introductory courses in the sciences often are competitive, selective, and intimidating. Instructors rarely attempt to recruit students to the discipline or to create a sense of community among them. As a result, many students sense that they are part of a group for whom there is no room in science.

In motivating more minorities to pursue careers in science, Uri Triesman, a mathematician at the University of Texas hailed for his pioneering work in teaching, underscores the importance of organizing "around the culture of science, not just ethnic identity" (Gibbons, 1992b). Studies show that a critical factor for minority students' academic success in math and the sciences is studying and discussing academic issues with other students outside class, rather than working alone and separating their academic and social lives.

Value on Diversity

The committee advocates that diversity becomes prized as a resource, characterized by genuine respect for students' varying backgrounds, talents, and learning styles.

As emphasized in this report, diversity is a resource, a criterion for excellence, as our nation moves to a new stage of economic and scientific development. By the year 2020, 40 percent of America's youth will be members of minority groups (Nickens, 1992). America cannot afford to ignore the brainpower and potential contributions of the fastest growing segments of its citizenry. All programs directed at broadening the educational pathway must do better in reaching out to students, parents, and communities of all racial and ethnic groups. Institutions at all levels should be strongly encouraged to move beyond formal requirements to emphasize the value of the unique attributes of each individual. Schools need to create and foster attractive oases of learning that both engender respect and celebrate multiculturalism and diversity.

The Right Attitude for Learning

Educational institutions at all levels must promulgate the principle that "smart isn't something you are, it's something you can become."

The perception that educational attainment in math and science is directly related to innate ability, rather than to hard work and committed effort, is challenged in a number of recent studies and surveys. A new National Urban League study indicates that intellectual development is not dependent on special innate gifts, but is more the result of hard work and organized effort (Howard, 1993). Similarly, another analysis comparing achievement in mathematics of Chinese, Japanese, and American children over a decade, showed that heightened emphasis on math and science education had little influence on academic achievement and parental attitudes (Stevenson et al., 1993). The survey indicated that U.S. parents appear satisfied with an educational system that continues to underperform because they believe, counter to the Chinese and Japanese, that innate ability, rather than effort and seriousness of purpose, determines proficiency in the math and sciences. The author concludes that the U.S. achievement gap is unlikely to diminish until, among other things, there are marked changes in the attitudes and beliefs of American parents and students about education and the contribution of hard work and effort to academic success.

Culturally Sensitive Communications

Commitment to diversity must be associated with heightened sensitivity and respect for cultural differences. Special efforts should be made to foster improved communication and understanding among diverse groups, working together toward common goals.

This report emphasizes the importance of valuing diversity as a positive human resource. Each component, every building block of any strategic plan targeted to enhancing career opportunities for minorities in medicine, must reflect this principle. Even a small investment in developing a more hospitable, inclusive environment for learning may yield significant gains in furthering the academic careers of individuals.

Research indicates that well-intentioned educational enrichment programs may fail in part because of poor communication among minority students, particularly between African Americans and teachers or faculty. A number of studies indicate that, in most cases, the academic problems of minority students are remedial and transient (Fullilove et al., 1988; Action Council on Minority Education, 1990; Kahn, 1992). Many problems are actually problems of acculturation to the medical school environment and reflect the inability of the medical school to integrate a racially diverse student body. A failure of acculturation is likely to have a strong effect on grades (Fullilove et al., 1988). For example, in considering student learning difficulties, faculty members tend to focus on cognitive factors such as background preparation, reading, and communication skills. Students, considering the same difficulties, may emphasize issues such as trust, liking, and bias. An institution's or faculty member's focus on "qualified" students may be seen as a discriminatory or biased attitude by minority students who lack the assurance and sense of self-worth that contribute so vitally to a sense of empowerment and confidence to succeed.

Encouraging minorities to pursue more advanced study in the sciences will require improving the "climate" of the classroom. All students must be made to feel they are truly valued and they can achieve academic success. This includes valuing of their culture and language and the appreciation of their individual talents. As emphasized in Chapter 2, often there is too little recognition that the inadequacies of the early education encountered by many minority students leave them ill-prepared for a highly competitive environment.

Mentorship

The committee believes in the central role of mentoring, with its proven ability to help minorities achieve their career goals. Mentoring must become a structured component of programs dedicated to achieving a larger presence of minorities in the health professions.

Minorities who have stayed the educational course often credit someone—a parent, teacher, or mentor—for helping them succeed. In assessing past efforts, the committee concluded that **two critical components of successful programs are good teaching and mentoring, offered in a systematic way to students of all ages.** Mentors guide, inform, and illuminate the way toward higher educational achievement; they help traverse the academic maze. Mentoring releases talent and energy that would otherwise lie dormant. Data, however, show that only one in eight African Americans during their graduate and professional education has ever had a true mentor (Blackwell, 1989). Lack of access to an advisor and mentor, minority or otherwise, can be a crucial barrier to developing minority faculty and minority academic leadership.

Mentoring is time consuming and often neither appreciated nor adequately rewarded. Many minority faculty members, especially at majority institutions, believe they are penalized for spending too much time with students, who may indeed make extraordinary demands on their time (Blackwell, 1989).

The scarcity of minority role models and mentors among practicing health professionals and in academe contributes to the problem of attracting minority students to the health professions and reinforces the perception that it is probably unrealistic for minority youngsters to consider this career option. Minority medical faculty have an important influence on both the number and the quality of minority students (Wilson, 1992).

The committee supports the new emphasis that many mentoring organizations are placing on outreach, training, support for mentors, and thoughtful matching of mentors and students. **Ongoing commitment to mentoring requires a solid program infrastructure at the institutional level.** In order not to place an undue burden on a few individuals within an institution, steps might be considered to develop a mentor-rich environment that brings minority youths into open, trusting relationships with a variety of role models and supportive professionals.

Improved Evaluation and Dissemination Efforts

Collection and timely dissemination of better data and tracking systems to measure progress should be developed. All programs must be strongly encouraged to incorporate an evaluation and reporting component. Successful elements of recruitment and retention programs should be collected and published on a regular basis and disseminated to all institutions responsible for health professions training, beginning with high school. Capacity building in this arena will help these institutions identify and learn from the most promising and effective interventions as well as documenting those that are not working.

Major obstacles can be eliminated by expanding or replicating existing successful intervention models. Nationwide there are successful programs, but many are overlooked as a result of lack of documentation and publication. There needs to be increasing emphasis on timely dissemination of evaluation findings in a format that can be used by all the various constituencies involved in these efforts.

The committee found that only a few programs have been rigorously assessed or publicly evaluated. Programs to promote minorities in science are often managed with little oversight or accountability. Fragmentary evidence and few solid, supporting data have handicapped program assessment, the documentation of program success, and broader replication of promising efforts (Sims, 1992; Epps et al., 1993). Few assessments of the effectiveness of intervention programs in optometry, dentistry, veterinary medicine, podiatry, and nursing have been widely published (Epps et al., 1993).

Broader use of case-controlled studies to develop better information on what does and does not work in helping minorities advance through the health careers educational process should been encouraged. Such studies could strengthen the knowledge base, documenting what interventions are most effective in helping minorities achieve success in medicine and science.

The committee recommends that a national information network and clearinghouse be developed that provides timely information on activities relevant to minority health professionals.

Such a network would prove invaluable to students, faculty, and administrators. Once established, its availability should be widely advertised. Students, faculty, and mentors would be encouraged both to use it and to contribute to ongoing exchange of information. The use of electronic media and interactive communications to disseminate the latest data about educational opportunities, special programs, and financial aid would contribute significantly to broadening the interest and information base in this area.

Improved, Coordinated Resources

Further efforts to improve the targeting, coordination and administration of federal programs directed at minority health can help ensure the most effective use of scarce federal dollars. Similarly, the growing importance of states and localities in health care reform, health professions education, and health workforce policies calls for the federal government to work more closely with states and their respective academic communities in order to develop a health professions workforce responsive to the needs of different regions and populations. Leading health professions organizations such as the AMA and ADA, with sizeable national and statewide networks, also can play an important role in improving the coordination and dissemination of public and private activities in this arena.

The committee suggests that federal funding increasingly reflect the importance of supporting programs that improve the size and quality of the minority applicant pool by focusing on early interventions.

Federal funds must continue to be made available to those schools with demonstrated excellence in educating minority students. Minority schools such as Howard, Meharry, and Morehouse struggle for financial survival while remaining responsible for the successful training and mentorship of a disproportionate share of underrepresented minority students. Incentives and rewards also should be directed at those academic health science centers willing to develop concerted efforts to increase the ranks of minority students and faculty.

A cohesive, strategic framework for broadening the pipeline for minorities in the health professions can make more effective use of existing resources. Some surveys of past efforts suggest that the survival of effective special programs is often due less to external funding than to sustained commitment by institutions of learning and other community organizations devoted to a greater minority presence (Huckman and Rattenbury, 1992; Epps et al., 1993). Nevertheless, the administration's stated objective of developing a more diverse health professions workforce as a key component of national health care reform and broadening access will require additional, well-targeted public resources.

The availability of student financial assistance must be ensured through public and private sector scholarships. More research is needed to assess the impact of rising tuition costs and a growing debt burden on the desire and ability of underrepresented minorities to consider medical school.

The high cost of medical education may be a critical factor constraining the size of the minority applicant pool and may make the more immediate financial rewards of other career paths more attractive (Ginzberg et al., 1993). Outstanding debt for indebted medical school graduates has grown significantly over the past 15 years, the result of major tuition increases and a decline in the availability of scholarships (Hughes et al., 1991). In 1992, the overall average debt of indebted medical students was over $55,000, and it was more than $58,000 for underrepresented minority students (AAMC [Association of American Medical Colleges], 1993a).

It has been shown that students actively sought by many medical schools—those from families with low incomes and from underrepresented minority groups, who are often also from poor families—end up with the most debt. Young African-American physicians have substantially more debt than young white physicians even after parental social class and level of tuition are taken into account. To the extent that debt is an economic and psychological burden, medical schools are in the paradoxical position of increasing constraints on the very students they seek to help (Hughes et al., 1991).

A number of well-known researchers and leaders in the medical field have raised the notion that the federal government should finance medical education in exchange for a universal public service, the requirement to practice in a high-need area for a certain number of years (Hughes et al., 1991; Ginzberg et al., 1993; Petersdorf, 1993). The consideration of such a fundamental change in medical school financing remains an issue of lively debate. Short of compulsory service, however, the voluntary National Health Service Corps has much to be commended, particularly as it relates to broadening opportunities for those students who are less financially able to pursue a medical career.

Resources should be directed at faculty development, curricular revision, and program support for success in achieving greater minority participation at the university level.

Successful strategies at the academic level require faculty time, initiative, innovation, and leadership. They require resources for faculty development, curricular revision, and program support, as well as meaningful incentives for faculty who participate. While universities, as well as other educational institutions, can appeal to the humanitarian impulses of faculty by asking them to be more alert for opportunities to improve the academic climate for minority students and faculty, **appeals to altruistic values work best when accompanied by rewards and sanctions.**

The university environment, however, is competing increasingly for a diminishing pool of financial resources. The time has passed when a dean or a department head could simply start a new division or hire added staff to meet the demands for curricular change. Almost every initiative must be matched with a reduction or elimination in another area. Academic health centers, however, through their development offices have a unique opportunity to solicit extramural funding for diversity efforts. This may generate corporate support to attract minority youth to worksites, research units, and professional educational opportunities only a health science center can generate. Today's economic climate underscores the **critical importance of heightening, at all levels, the institutional commitment to minority health professions training and the priority this issue is given by those who make funding decisions.**

Improving Health Services for Minorities

Health care reform should recognize and promote opportunities both for greater minority participation in the health professions and for better health services for minority populations.

The importance and relevance of the committee's deliberations in this arena gain added impetus from today's strong national focus on health care reform and its stated goal of developing a health professions workforce more responsive to America's increasing diversity and changing health care needs. In anticipation of national reform, major changes in health care financing and delivery are being unveiled, not only at the federal level but also in the states and the corporate community. High on the reform agenda are plans for universal access, preventive care, and increased reimbursement and recognition for primary care. These changes should make it more attractive to serve currently underserved populations, usually composed of a disproportionate number of disadvantaged minorities. Heightened attractiveness, prestige, and financial awards for primary care will benefit minority physicians who have been more likely in the past to select this specialty (Council on Graduate Medical Education, 1992; Hopkins, 1992; Fox, 1993). Further, the discipline of primary care and general medicine is gaining increasing respect within academe as it fosters new, rich areas of clinical investigation, health services research, and related activities.

There is also an urgent need to attract more minority physicians to academic medicine and research.

The career pathways of practitioner, researcher, and teacher should not be in competition with each other. Underrepresentation in the health professions is even more disturbing when one looks at the paltry number of minority faculty members in medical schools. A minority faculty member in a leadership position often provides the atmosphere conducive to the recruitment, development, and retention of minority staff and faculty (Wilson, 1992; Epps et al., 1993).

Minority students should be exposed to meaningful research experiences early in their academic careers, as early as at the high school level. Such an exposure could broaden the pool of individuals potentially interested in research and teaching positions, as well as contribute to success in the health professions. In addition, minority researchers can contribute significantly to research and understanding of special conditions that contribute to poor health among minorities.

MOVING THE VISION FORWARD

How best to realize the vision for a more diversified health workforce was the central theme of the workshop conducted as part of the committee's deliberation. The 24 attendees were invited on the basis of their accomplishments, creativity, and broad perspectives in the fields of education, community development, governance, and health professions training. Many of those at the meeting had made significant contributions to the field of minority education and advancement. Through an intense, interactive process, the workshop identified several strategies described in the preceding pages that hold promise for providing the extra energy, visibility, and commitment that help bring a vision closer to reality. The committee developed blueprints for intensive but broadly based community initiatives, outlined strategies for enhancing the minority presence in academic health centers, and considered multimedia campaigns that could help capture and convey the excitement and rewards of a health professions career to minority youth.

Community-Wide Initiative

The committee recommends that foundations, through a number of demonstration projects, sponsor communities that develop their own comprehensive plan for systematic reform and implement a dynamic, multifaceted community effort directed at minority health professions training, together with a goals statement and implementation plan.

For the vision to succeed, the nation must look beyond its schools and institutions, to its communities and families. The formal education system alone cannot improve the problem of persistent underrepresentation. Future efforts will require a higher level of support among parents and all community-based leaders and organizations that contribute to education, health careers, mentoring, and the promotion of cultural diversity. Strategies that build on the strengths of community identity and culture are more likely to succeed than those imposed externally. **Each community must become a place where learning can happen, a place that produces children equipped to make a wide array of choices and to succeed in the choices they make.**

The committee envisions community efforts that involve institutions of learning from elementary schools through graduate training, churches, business leaders, health care organizations and providers, and other relevant stakeholders. Major emphasis would be placed on hands-on experience, outreach, and sustained mentoring from health professionals, ranging from the physician in private practice, to the rehabilitation counselor, to the visiting nurse, to the community's leading researchers and health care administrators. A spectrum of activities would be developed and nourished, all directed to exposing minority youth and their families to the excitement, challenge, and satisfaction of pursuing a career in medicine or science. The expectation is that such community-based efforts will raise the quality and environment for science teaching, attract additional resources, and make the prospect of a health or science career a stimulating, rewarding, and feasible career pathway. **The committee believes that this kind of coordinated effort can bring about lasting changes in the attitude and behavior of the community.**

A significant component of the community initiative would be a structured grass-roots mentoring program, using the economic, financial, and social leverage of minority and nonminority individuals who have achieved professional standing in their neighborhoods. Many minority individuals who have been successful would welcome an opportunity to share the benefits of their experiences with future generations. These individuals would develop a structured program directed at reaching out and developing the capacities of the "farm team," youngsters considering health careers who could benefit from ongoing support and practical advice. **The committee believes that funding for such demonstration programs should come from a combination of governmental, business, and philanthropic agencies and individuals.**

The committee recommends that a national information network and clearinghouse be developed that provides timely information on activities relevant to minority health professionals.

The committee believes that such a network would prove invaluable to students, faculty, and administrators. The use of electronic media and interactive communications to disseminate the latest data about educational opportunities, special programs, and financial aid would contribute significantly to broadening the interest and information base in this area. The availability of such a network should be widely advertised. Students, faculty, and mentors should be encouraged not only to use it but also to contribute to ongoing exchange of information.

The committee recommends that the federal government, the foundation world, and the private sector support an annual workshop and ongoing activities devoted to furthering the art of mentoring in the health professions.

Mentoring has proved to be a critical component of successful voyages through the health professions educational pipeline. Numerous mentoring organizations now exist; many are engaged in efforts that have garnered considerable success. However, more often than not, these kinds of activities are thinly funded. Much could be gained from providing an enrichment opportunity for individuals seriously engaged in mentoring to meet and learn from those who have developed especially effective programs.

Commitment and Initiatives of Academic Health Centers

The committee recommends that academic health centers set a higher priority toward enhanced minority participation and maintain a high level of sustained commitment to this goal. The committee encourages academic health centers to forge partnerships with major corporations and other educational entities targeted to building programs to attract and support youths interested in the health professions.

Over the years, many of the nation's academic health centers and the Association of Academic Medical Colleges have made impressive contributions to advancing minorities in health careers. Several schools, with large minority constituency, have had a particularly striking impact. A promising new AAMC initiative, "Project 3000 by 2000," includes many elements of the desired strategic actions endorsed by the committee. The project's principal objective is to form partnerships linking academic medical centers with undergraduate colleges, local high school systems, and community organizations. Despite such worthy efforts, however, little evidence suggests significant priorities and strategies of most medical schools to increase minority enrollment and faculty development. Many programs have been established as "additions" to ongoing efforts, but they have never become part of the central, sustained mission of these institutions.

If the leadership of a medical school decides to make minority enrollment and faculty development a top priority, that school is likely to improve its record in this area. Instituting meaningful incentives and sanctions to promote desired outcomes, assigning staff time, and appointing high-level administrators to focus on this area are signs that institutions are serious about enhancing the presence of minorities in the nation's health care enterprise.

The committee recommends that community service and outreach become a fourth component of an academic health center's mission, in addition to teaching, research, and patient care. Similarly, the committee joins others in recommending formal inclusion of some level of community service among the criteria for academic recognition and advancement, in addition to the time-honored measures of scholarly and clinical achievement.

Academic health centers need increasingly to form community partnerships with local schools and colleges to nurture the curiosity and develop the talents of students who may have an interest in health careers. They need to reach out further to care for the underserved. They need to study health and illness in the community setting. Faculty leading and joining in such efforts often gain little recognition from the traditional academic reward systems. Implementing the committee recommendation would rapidly bring to academe a new sense of priority for community-based initiatives.

The Media and Health Careers

The committee calls on the corporate sector to develop and support multimedia campaigns to attract youngsters into the health professions. The committee suggests that relevant regulatory organizations within the communications industry establish a time bank, into which a defined percentage of all radio and TV time periods be deposited. Its objective would be to reserve a portion of America's public voice for social priorities.

The imperative to enhance diversity in the health professions needs a more public voice. The media and their leaders can play a key role in creating a critical mass of support for turning minority youth "on" to science and careers in medicine. Many educators have observed that children are born scientists, endlessly questioning where things come from and how they work. The media and those who develop advertising campaigns can help educate minority youth about the fun, prestige, challenge, and rewards, both financial and emotional, associated with careers in science and medicine. Leading sports and entertainment figures, idolized by America's youth, could be enlisted to help attract minorities to careers in medicine. For example, a prominent rock star could talk about his experience with the health care system, recovering from a serious illness or an accident. A national basketball or football hero might describe the types of health care workers who helped him recover from a sports injury, commenting on their respective roles. Similarly, a leading sports or entertainment figure could talk about his battle with AIDS or another life-threatening disease and describe the kind of help and support he or she is receiving from various members of the health care team. A famous pop singer might talk about the health professions from the perspective of having to help care for a chronically ill family member. These kind of public service announcements, designed both to educate and to motivate, could help promulgate the message that a career in the health professions is rewarding, exciting, and within reach. Combining such an effort with the community-wide initiatives described above might prove synergistic and have notable impact.

SUMMARY

The committee's recommendations underscore the need to encourage continued experimentation, particularly with programs that emphasize integrated, community-based actions and sustained commitments. Strategies that include community involvement may best be able to address the spectrum of disincentives—economic, educational, social, cultural, and attitudinal—that today deter minorities from careers in medicine and science. This agenda calls for bold and demanding measures. To achieve them will take patience, persistence, and flexibility. The vision of equal opportunity and participation of all citizens of the United States deserves nothing less.

References

Action Council on Minority Education. *Education That Works: An Action Plan for the Education of Minorities.* Cambridge, Mass.: Massachusetts Institute of Technology, 1990.

American Dental Association Commission on the Young Professional. Tomorrow's ADA: Responding to the Challenge of Diversity. *A Portrait of Minority and Women Dentists.* Washington, D.C.: American Dental Association, 1992.

American Health Security Act. Washington, D.C.: U.S. Government Printing Office, 1993.

AMA (American Medical Association) Council on Ethical and Judicial Affairs. Black-White Disparities in Health Care. *Journal of the American Medical Association* 253(17):2344-2346, 1990.

AMA Council on Scientific Affairs. Hispanic Health in the United States. *Journal of the American Medical Association* 265(2):248-252, 1991.

Angell, M. Privilege and Health—What Is the Connection? *The New England Journal of Medicine* 329(2):126-127, 1993.

AAMC (Association of American Medical Colleges). *Report of the Association of American Medical Colleges Task Force on Minority Student Opportunities in Medicine.* Washington, D.C.: AAMC, 1978.

AAMC. *Minority Students in Medical Education: Facts and Figures VII.* Washington, D.C.: AAMC, 1993a.

AAMC. Report to the Commonwealth Fund and National Medical Fellowships, Inc.: Tracking Commonwealth Fund Fellows. Washington, D.C.: AAMC, 1993b.

Baratz, J.C., Ficklin, B., King, B., et al. *Who Is Going to Medical School? A Look at the 1984-85 Underrepresented Minority Medical School Applicant Pool.* Princeton, N.J.: Educational Testing Service, 1985.

Billings, J. and Teicholz, N. Uninsured Patients in the District of Columbia. *Health Affairs* 9(4):158-165, 1990.

Blackwell, J.E. Mentoring: An Action Strategy for Increasing Minority Faculty. *Academe* 75(5):8-14, 1989.

REFERENCES

Bureau of the Health Professions. Data reported by the individual health professions' associations. Washington, D.C.: U.S. Department of Health and Human Services, 1993.

Bush, V. *Science: "The Endless Frontier."* Washington, D.C.: Office of Scientific Research and Development, 1945.

Butler, W.T., Thomson, W.A., Morrissey, C.T., et al. Baylor's Program to Attract Minority Students and Others to Science and Medicine. *Academic Medicine* 66(6):305–311, 1991.

Carnegie Corporation. Ensuring Minorities' Success in Mathematics, Engineering, and Science: The MESA Program. *Carnegie Quarterly* 35(3,4):1–7, 1990.

Carter, D.J. and Wilson, R. *1992 Eleventh Annual Report on Minorities in Higher Education.* Washington, D.C.: American Council on Education, 1993.

Charles R. Drew University of Medicine and Science. *The Extended Science Pipeline Program.* 1992.

Chicago Area Health and Medical Careers Program. *An Overview: The Chicago Area Health and Medical Careers Program.* March 1992.

Cohen, A.B., Cantor, J.C., Barker, D.C., et al. Young Physicians and the Medical Profession. *Health Affairs* 9(4):138–148, 1990.

College Board. *Equality and Excellence: The Educational Status of Black Americans.* New York: College Entrance Examination Board, 1985.

Competitiveness Policy Council. *A Competitiveness Strategy for America: Second Report to the President and Congress.* Washington, D.C.: U.S. Government Printing Office, 1993.

COGME (Council on Graduate Medical Education). *Third Report.* Washington, D.C.: U.S. Department of Health and Human Services, 1992.

Cregler, L.L., Clark, L.T., and Jackson, E.B. Educational and Career Obstacles and Opportunities in Academic Medicine and Clinical Practice for Minorities: Is Progress Occurring? Paper prepared for the Institute of Medicine Study to Increase Minority Participation in the Health Professions, 1993.

Dougherty, C.J. Ethical Values at Stake in Health Care Reform. *Journal of the American Medical Association* 268(17):2409–2412, 1992.

Ebert, J.D. Science Education Reform: This Time, From Bottom Up. *National Research Council News Report* 42(3):19, 1993.

Edwards, J.C., Johnson, E.K., and Molidar, J.B. The Interview in the Admissions Process. *Academic Medicine* 65:167–177, 1990.

Edwards, J.N. Physician Characteristics and Minority Health Care Use. Proposal to the Association for Health Care Policy and Research, forthcoming.

Epps, A.C., Cureton-Russell, M.T., and Kitzman, H.G.H. The Problem of Underrepresentation and an Inventory and Analysis of Effective Strategies and Programs. Paper prepared for the Institute of Medicine Study to Increase Minority Participation in the Health Professions, 1993.

Fox, M. Medical School Indebtedness and Choice of Specialization. *Inquiry* 30(Spring):84–94, 1993.

Fullilove, M.T., Fullilove, R.E., Terris, M., et al. Is Black Achievement an Oxymoron? *Thought and Action* 4(2):5–20, 1988.

Furino, A., ed. *Health Care Policy and the Hispanic.* Boulder, Colo.: Westview Press, 1992.

Geertsma, R.H. A Special Tutorial for Minority Medical Students: An Account of a Year's Experience. *Journal of Medical Education* 52:396–403, 1977.

Gibbons, A. Growing Scientists for the 21st Century. *Science* 258(13):1195, 1992a.

Gibbons, A. Minority Programs That Get High Marks. *Science* 258(13):1190–1196, 1992b.

Ginzberg, E. and Ostow, M. Beyond Universal Health Care to Effective Health Care. *Journal of the American Medical Association* 265:2559–2562, 1991.

Ginzberg, E. and Ostow, M. Physician Supply Strategy: The Case of the South. *Health Affairs* 11(2):193–197, 1992.

Ginzberg, E., Ostow, M., and Dutka, A.B. *The Economics of Medical Education.* New York: The Josiah Macy, Jr. Foundation, 1993.

Goldratt, E.M. and Cox, J. *The Goal: A Process of Ongoing Improvement. Revised Edition.* New York: North River Press, Inc., 1986.

Gore, A. *From Red Tape to Results: Creating a Government That Works Better and Costs Less, Report of the National Performance Review.* Washington, D.C.: Office of the Vice President, 1993.

HRSA (Health Resources and Services Administration). *Women and Minorities in the Health Fields.* Washington, D.C.: U.S. Department of Health and Human Services, 1990.

HRSA. Personal communication, October 6 and 7, 1993.

Healy, B. Address at the National Science Foundation's National Conference on Diversity in the Scientific and Technological Workforce. Washington, D.C., September 25–26, 1992.

Hopkins, J. U.S. Strives to Increase Ethnic Minorities in Medicine. *British Medical Journal* 304:1266, 1992.

Howard, J. The Third Movement: Developing Black Children for the 21st Century. In *The State of Black America.* Titwell, B., ed. Washington, D.C.: The National Urban League, 1993.

Huckman, B.B. and Rattenbury, B. The Need to Bring More Minority Students into Medicine. *American Medical News* 35(29):26, 1992.

Hughes, R.G., Barker, D.C., and Reynolds, R.C. Are We Mortgaging the Health Profession? *The New England Journal of Medicine* 325(6):404–407, 1991.

IOM (Institute of Medicine). *Prenatal Care: Reaching Mothers, Reaching Infants.* Brown, S., ed. Washington, D.C.: National Academy Press, 1988.

IOM. *Allied Health Services: Avoiding Crises.* Washington, D.C.: National Academy Press, 1989.

IOM. *Healthy People 2000: Citizens Chart the Course.* Stoto, M., Behrens, R. and Rosemont, C., eds. Washington, D.C.: National Academy Press, 1990.

IOM. *Access to Health Care in America.* Millman, M., ed. Washington, D.C.: National Academy Press, 1993.

Jennings, J. Race and Excellence in American Higher Education. *Trotter Institute Review* 3(3):7–12, 1989.

REFERENCES

Johnson, D.G., Smith, V.C., and Tarnoff, S.L. Recruitment and Progress of Minority Medical School Entrants: 1970-1972. *Journal of Medical Education* 50:713k-755, 1975.

Johnson, L., Jr. Financing Medical Education for Minorities: "Debt" It's Not the Problem. *Journal of the National Medical Student Association* 2(2):24-27, 1990.

Jolley, P. and Hudley, D.M. *AAMC Data Book: Statistical Information Related to Medical Education.* Washington, D.C.: AAMC, 1993.

Kahn, S. University Science Teaching Must Reach Out to Women and Minorities. *The Journal of NIH Research* 4(1):56-60, 1992.

King, M.L., Jr. *Chaos or Community: Where Do We Go From Here.* Boston, Mass.: Beacon Press, 1967.

Leff, L. Smoothing the Rough Road to a Doctorate in Science. *Washington Post*, May 4:B1, 1993.

Matyas, M.L. and Malcom, S.M. *Women, Minorities, and Persons with Physical Disabilities in Science and Engineering.* Washington, D.C.: American Association for the Advancement of Science, 1991.

Mitchell, K.J. Use of MCAT Data in Selecting Students for Admission to Medical School. *Journal of Medical Education* 62(11):871-879, 1987.

Mullis, I.Z.S. and Jenkins, L.B. The Science Report Card: Trends and Achievements Based on the 1986 Assessment. Report no.: 17-S-01. Educational Testing Service, 1988.

Munoz, E., Tortella, B.J., Sakmyster, M.A., et al. Traumatic Injury in Hispanic Americans: A Distinct Entity. In *Health Care Policy and the Hispanic.* Furino, A., ed. Boulder, Colo.: Westview Press, 1992.

National Center for Health Statistics. *Vital Statistics of the United States, 1989: Volume II.* Washington, D.C.: Public Health Service, 1992.

NRC (National Research Council). *A Common Destiny: Blacks and American Society.* Washington, D.C.: National Academy Press, 1989.

NSF (National Science Foundation). *Blacks in Undergraduate Science and Engineering Education.* Washington, D.C.: National Science Foundation, 1992.

Nickens, H.W. The Rationale for Minority-Targeted Programs in Medicine in the 1990s. *Journal of the American Medical Association* 267(17):2390-2395, 1992.

Odegaard, C.E. *Minorities in Medicine: From Receptive Passivity to Positive Action, 1966-1976.* New York: The Josiah Macy, Jr., Foundation, 1977.

Pappas, G., Queen, S., Hadden, W. et al. The Increasing Disparity in Mortality Between Socioeconomic Groups in the United States, 1960 and 1986. *The New England Journal of Medicine* 329(2):103-109, 1993.

Pelavin, S.H. and Kane M. *Changing the Odds: Factors Increasing Access to College.* New York: College Entrance Examination Board, 1990.

Petersdorf, R.G. Financing Medical Education: A Universal "Berry Plan" for Medical Students. *The New England Journal of Medicine* 328(9):651-654, 1993.

Petersdorf, R.G. *Not a Choice, An Obligation.* Paper presented at the Plenary Session of the 102nd Meeting of the Association of American Medical Colleges. Washington, D.C.: AAMC, 1991.

Petersdorf, R.G. et al. Minorities in Medicine: Past, Present, and Future. *Academic Medicine* 65(11):663-670, 1990.

Pico, E., Wimbley, M., and Wells, K.B. First Year Students' Expectations of Interacting with Minority Patients and Colleagues. *Academic Medicine* 67(6):411–412, 1992.

Quality Education Project. *Education That Works: An Action Plan for the Education of Minorities.* Cambridge, Mass.: Massachusetts Institute of Technology, 1990.

Ratchford, T. Human Resources in Science and Technology. Proceedings of the Commission on Professionals in Science and Technology, March 26–27, 1992, pp. 59–67.

Ready, T.P. and Nickens, H.W. Inventory and Analysis of the Effectiveness of Strategies and Programs for Increasing Minority Participation in Medicine. Paper prepared for the Institute of Medicine Study to Increase Minority Participation in the Health Professions, 1993.

Ready, T.P. and Nickens, H.W. The Underrepresentation Problem: Minorities in the Health Professions. Menlo Park, Calif.: Kaiser Family Foundation, forthcoming.

Reed, W.L., Darity, W., Roman, S., Baquet, C. et al. *The Health and Medical Care of African Americans.* Boston, Mass.: William Monroe Trotter Institute, 1992.

Reitzes, D.C. and Elkhanialy, H. Black Students in Medical Schools. *Journal of Medical Education* 51:1001–1005, 1976.

Richardson, R.C. and Skinner, E.F. *Achieving Quality and Diversity: Universities in a Multicultural Society.* New York: American Council on Education and Macmillan Publishing Company, 1991.

Robert Wood Johnson Foundation. *Special Report: The Foundation's Minority Medical Training Programs.* Princeton, N.J.: The Robert Wood Johnson Foundation Communications Office, 1987.

Schroeder, S.A., Zones, J.S., and Showstack, J.A. Academic Medicine as a Public Trust. *Journal of the American Medical Association* 262(6):803–812, 1989.

Sedlacek, W.E. Black Students on White Campuses: 20 Years of Research. *Journal of College Student Personnel* 28(6):484–495, 1987.

Selvin, P. Math Education: Multiplying the Meager Numbers. *Science* 258(13):1200–1201, 1992.

Shea, S. and Fullilove, M.T. Entry of Minority Students into U.S. Medical Schools: Historical Perspective and Recent Trends. *The New England Journal of Medicine* 313(15):933–940, 1985.

Simpson, C.E. and Aronoff, R. Factors Affecting the Supply of Minority Physicians in 2000. *Public Health Reports* 103(2):178–184, 1988.

Sims, C. What Went Wrong: Why Programs Failed. *Science* 258(13):1185–1187, 1992.

Smith, M.O. Health Personnel in a Diverse Society. In *Human Resources for Health: Defining the Future.* Evarts, C.M., Bosomworth, P.P., and Osterweis, M., eds. Washington, D.C.: Association of Academic Health Centers, 1992.

Stanfield, R.L. Black Frustration. *National Journal* 24(20):1162–1166, 1992.

Starfield, B. Primary Care and Health: A Cross-National Comparison. *Journal of the American Medical Association* 266(16):2268–2271, 1991.

Steele, C.M. Race and the Schooling of Black Americans. *Atlantic Monthly* 269(10):68, 1992.

Stevenson, H.W., Chuansheng, C., and Shin-Ying, L. Mathematics Achievement of Chinese, Japanese, and American Children: Ten Years Later. *Science* 259(5091):53–58, 1993.

REFERENCES

Taylor, R.E., Jr., Hunt, J.C., and Temple, P. Recruiting Black Medical Students: A Decade of Effort. *Academic Medicine* 65(5):279–288, 1990.

U.S. Bureau of the Census. *The 1990 Decennial Census.* Washington, D.C.: U.S. Bureau of the Census, 1990.

U.S. Department of Education. *Trends in Enrollment in Higher Education by Racial/Ethnic Category: Fall 1982 Through Fall 1991.* Washington, D.C.: U.S. Department of Education, 1991.

U.S. Department of Health and Human Services. *Report of the Secretary's Task Force on Black and Minority Health: Volume I.* Washington, D.C.: U.S. Government Printing Office, 1985.

Weinberg, M. *A Chance to Learn: A History of Race and Education.* London: Cambridge University Press, 1977.

Western Interstate Commission for Higher Education and the College Board. *The Road to College: Educational Progress by Race and Ethnicity.* Boulder, Colo.: Western Interstate Commission for Higher Education, 1991.

Whittle, J., Conigliaro, J., Goode, C.B., et al. Racial Differences in the Use of Invasive Cardiovascular Procedures in the Department of Veterans Affairs Medical System. *The New England Journal of Medicine* 329(9):621–627, 1993.

Wilson, D.E. The Need for Minority Role Models in Academic Medicine. *The Fellowship Program in Academic Medicine for Minority Students Newsletter* Spring:1–2, 1992.

Wilson, D.E. and Kaczmarek, J.M. The History of African American Physicians and Medicine in the United States. *Journal of the Association of Academic Minority Physicians* 4(3), 1993.

Wolkon, G.H. and Yamamoto, J. Medical Student Attitudes About Quality of Care and Training. *Journal of the National Medical Association* 79:185–186, 1978.

A

Listing of Workshop Participants and Commissioned Papers

WORKSHOP PARTICIPANTS

Billy Ballard, M.D.
Associate Dean for Student Affairs
and Admissions
University of Texas Medical School
Galveston, Texas

Bruce L. Ballard, M.D.
Associate Dean
Student Affairs
Equal Opportunity Program
Cornell Medical College
New York, New York

Katherine Flores, M.D.
Program Director
Border Area Health Education
 (AHEC) Council
Border AHEC System
Fresno, California

Henry W. Foster, Jr., M.D.
Dean, School of Medicine
Vice President for Health Services
Meharry Medical College
Nashville, Tennessee

Bruce Goldman
Executive Director
Harlem Hospital Center
New York, New York

Marian L. Heard
President and
Chief Executive Officer
United Way, Massachusetts Bay
Boston, Massachusetts

Milton Hernandez, M.D.
National Institutes of Health
Bethesda, Maryland

Carlos M. Interian, D.M.D.
Private Practitioner
Miami, Florida

Billy E. Jones, M.D., M.S.
President
New York City Health and
 Hospitals Corporation
New York, New York

APPENDIX A

Regnal J. Jones, Ph.D.
Executive Director
Chicago Area Health and Medical
 Careers Program
Chicago, Illinois

Stephen N. Keith, M.D.
Senior Customer Manger
Merck & Co., Inc.
West Point, Pennsylvania

Herbert Nickens, M.D.
Vice President
Division of Minority Health,
 Education, and Prevention
Association of American
 Medical Colleges
Washington, D.C.

Elena Rios, M.D., M.S.P.H.
President
Chicano/Latino Medical Association
 of California
Office of Statewide Health Planning
 and Development
Sacramento, California

Barbara Ross-Lee, D.O.
Dean
Ohio College of Osteopathic
 Medicine
Athens, Ohio

Sheila A. Ryan, Ph.D., R.N., FAAN
Dean, School of Nursing
Director, Medical Center Nursing
University of Rochester
Rochester, New York

Al Siu, M.D., M.S.P.H.
Assistant Professor
Department of Medicine
University of California,
 Los Angeles
Los Angeles, California

Morton Slater, Ph.D.
Mt. Sinai School of Medicine
New York, New York

Gloria R. Smith, Ph.D.
Coordinator of Health Programs
W.K. Kellogg Foundation
Battle Creek, Michigan

William A. Thomson, Ph.D.
Head
Division of School-Based Programs
Baylor College of Medicine
Houston, Texas

Reed Tuckson, M.D.
President
Charles Drew University
Los Angeles, California

Margaret Daniels Tyler, Ph.D.
Dean in Residence
Council of Graduate Schools
Washington, D.C.

Norma E. Wagoner, Ph.D.
Dean of Students
University of Chicago
Pritzger School of Medicine
Chicago, Illinois

Luther S. Williams, Ph.D.
Assistant Director
Education and Human Resources
National Science Foundation
Washington, D.C.

Donald E. Wilson, M.D.
Dean
University of Maryland
School of Medicine
Baltimore, Maryland

COMMISSIONED PAPERS

The Institute of Medicine's Committee on Increasing Minority Participation in the Health Professions commissioned three papers for the April 1993 workshop. Participants used the papers as guides and background to their discussions. Copies of the papers may be obtained from the authors.

- "Inventory and Analysis of the Effectiveness of Strategies and Programs for Increasing Minority Participation in Medicine" by Timothy Ready and Herbert Nickens.
- "Educational and Career Obstacles and Opportunities in Academic Medicine and Clinical Practice for Priorities: Is Progress Occurring?" by Louis Cregler, Luther Clark, and Edgar Jackson.
- "Increasing Minority Participation in the Health Profession—The Problem of Underrepresentation and an Inventory and Analysis of Effective Strategies and Programs" by A. Cherrie Epps, Mary Cureton-Russell, and Helen Kitzman.

B

Further Sources of Information

REFERENCES

Black Issues in Higher Education
Biweekly publication.
Frank Matthews, Publisher
Cox, Matthews & Associates, 1993

Education That Works: An Action Plan for the Education of Minorities
Quality Education Project
Massachusetts Institute of Technology, 1990

HCOP Digest
Bureau of Health Professions
Division of Disadvantaged Assistance
U.S. Department of Health and Human Services, 1993

Research Training and Career Development Programs
National Institutes of Health, 1992

Technical Assistance Manual: Guidelines for Action
Project 3000 by 2000
Association of American Medical Colleges, 1992

The Underrepresentation Problem: Minorities in the Health Professions Part II: Review of Current Programs and Future Directions
Association of American Medical Colleges, 1992

PROGRAMS

More Minorities in the Health Professions
The Henry J. Kaiser Family Foundation
Quadras, 2400 Sand Hill Road
Menlo Park, California 94025   (415) 854-9400
The Foundation has established several demonstration and evaluation projects across the country. The programs support efforts to improve middle and high school students' academic and social preparation for college, and provide students with early and sustained exposure to health issues and health professionals.

National Association for Equal Opportunity in Higher Education
Black Higher Education Center
400 12th Street, NE
Washington, DC 20002   (202) 543-9111
Undergraduate umbrella organization for historically black colleges and universities. Distributes information on minority scholarships to member schools.

National Center for the Advancement of Blacks
   in the Health Professions
P.O. Box 21121
Detroit, Michigan 48221   (313) 345-4480
Collects, analyzes, and disseminates information about the underrepresentation of African Americans in the health professions. Conducts retreats and symposia for members. Produces a monthly newsletter, "Pathways to Parity."

National Hispanic Mentor Recruitment Network
Interamerican College of Physicians and Surgeons
U.S. Public Health Service
1101 15th Street, NW, Suite 502
Washington, DC 20005   (202) 467-4756
Serves as a resource for career development and residency program selection. Provides supportive role models, and offers a mechanism for obtaining financial information and career opportunities in the U.S. Public Health Service. Students are matched with physicians based on personal interests, practice setting medical specialty, and geographic location. Publishes a monthly newsletter, "Hispanics & Medicine."

National Institutes of Health
Division of Research Resources
5333 Westbard Avenue
Bethesda, Maryland 20892 (301) 496-6745
Offers scholarships and training programs for undergraduate and graduate students interested in biomedical research. Offers grants to minority faculty, K–graduate school.

National Science Foundation
Division of Human Resource Development
1800 G Street, NW
Washington, DC 20550 (202) 357-5052
Encourages minority science education and research through conferences, workshops, publications, and grants to institutions and individuals, K–graduate school.

Quality Education for Minorities Network
1818 N Street, NW, Suite 350
Washington, DC 20036 (202) 659-1818
National network to coordinate educational reform efforts, K–graduate school.

The Robert Wood Johnson Foundation
Route One and College Road
PO Box 2316
Princeton, New Jersey 08543 (609) 452-8701
Besides the Minority Medical Education Program discussed in Chapter 3, the Foundation supports the Minority Medical Faculty Development Program. The program offers up to twelve 4-year, postdoctoral research fellowships to underrepresented minority physicians.

Society for Advancement of Chicanos and Native Americans in Science
  (SACNAS)
Sinsheimer Laboratories
University of California
Santa Cruz, California 95064 (408) 459-4272
Serves students and professionals, K–graduate school. Holds annual meeting, offers outreach and workshops.